PAT RICHARDS CRAFTS COLLECTION

WONDERFUL

BABY QUILTS

TO MAKE

PAT RICHARDS CRAFTS COLLECTION

WONDERFUL

BABY QUILTS

TO MAKE

PAT RICHARDS

PHOTOGRAPHY BY GEORGE ROSS

FRIEDMAN/FAIRFAX
PUBLISHERS

A FRIEDMAN/FAIRFAX BOOK

© 1997 by Michael Friedman Publishing Group, Inc.

Library of Congress Cataloging-in-Publication Data

Richards, Pat, date
    Wonderful baby quilts to make / Pat Richards : photography
by George Ross.
        p.   cm. - - (The Pat Richards crafts collection)
Includes index.
ISBN 1-56799-400-8
1. Patchwork—Patterns.   2. Appliqué—Patterns.   2. Crib quilts.
I. Title.   II. Series: Richards, Pat,-Pat Richards crafts collection.
TT835.R533   1997
746.46'041—DC20   96-34083

Project Editor: Francine Hornberger
Editor: Jackie Smyth
Art Director: Jeff Batzli
Designer: Elan Studio
Photography Director: Christopher C. Bain
Production Manager: Jeanne Hutter
Photo Stylist: Karin Strom
Illustrator: Alan Andersen

All room photography © George Ross, except page 6, © Christopher C. Bain
Quilt copy photography by Christopher C. Bain

Additional credits: stuffed elephant and hat on page 2 from Toys on the Artic, Montclair, New Jersey; school bus and toy cars on pages 40–41, and all accessories on page 100 and 101 are from Jesse's Room, Montclair, New Jersey; the American Gothic Bunnies quilt was shot in the home of Ruth Bloom.

Color separations by Fine Arts Repro House Co., Ltd.
Printed in the United Kingdom by Butler & Tanner Limited

Every effort has been made to present the information in this book in a clear, complete, and accurate manner. It is important that all instructions be clearly understood before beginning a project. Please follow instructions carefully. Due to the variability of materials and skills, end results may vary. The publisher and author expressly disclaim any and all liability result-ing from injuries, damages, or other loss curred as a result of material presented herein. The author also suggests refraining from using glass, beads, or buttons on quilts intended for small children.

1 3 5 7 9 10 8 6 4 2

For bulk purchases and special sales, please contact:
Friedman/Fairfax Publishers
Attention: Sales Department
15 West 26th Street
New York, New York 10010
212/685-6610   FAX 212/685-1307

Visit our website:
http://www.metrobooks.com

This book is dedicated to my sons
Keith and Lee for whom I created my very first
baby quilts. Theirs soon came to be called magic
blankets, imbued with the power to keep away
bad dreams and bogeymen.

Thank you to my sister Amy Syrell who
has helped me out on a number of occasions.
On this book, she provided invaluable
assistance assembling the I, Robot, Airplanes,
and Squares on Squares quilts. Also of assistance
was Jackie Smyth who assembled the
Jungle Conga Line quilt and Michelle Filon
who assembled the Traffic Jam and
Toy Soldiers quilts.

CONTENTS

INTRODUCTION

When someone gets truly involved in a particular craft, it becomes a highly personalized process and they begin to develop their own methods of doing things. Quilting is very much like that: as you get into it you develop your favorite ways of cutting pieces, of assembling them, of quilting tops, attaching bindings, and so on. In this book I want to share with you some of the methods that have worked for me.

I've rated the projects in this book according to difficulty of assembly, designated by block symbols next to the quilt's dimensions. A one-block rating (✧) means a simple quilt. Two blocks (✧ ✧) mean a moderately challenging project. A project designated with three blocks (✧ ✧ ✧) is fairly intricate and should be tackled only by those with quilting experience and a fair amount of patience. You should always read through all the directions for each project before deciding whether or not to begin it.

After you've carefully read through the first chapter, you'll be ready to create your quilt for the special baby or toddler in your life. Create these quilts as they appear or make your own variations. Either way, your finished piece will be a treasured gift for years to come. Don't forget to sign it!

GETTING

CHAPTER ONE

STARTED

This section is designed to guide you through your quilting venture. Here, you will find tips on using materials and techniques. You will probably want to refer back to this section often while making your quilt.

PATTERNS

Because of the size of many of the pattern pieces used in this book, it was necessary to provide them in a scaled-down version. Some pieces may be easily enlarged at your local copy shop, but others—namely, the American Gothic Bunnies (page 39) and I, Robot (page 55)—will have to be drafted onto graph paper, which you can buy in rolls at your local art supply shop.

Depending on your preferences, the material you use to make your templates can be as basic as leftover cardboard or as specialized as the template plastic found in quilting shops. Template plastic does have an advantage in that you can see through it, making tracing patterns easier. Some patterns, particularly the appliqué ones, require using tracing paper. The generic sort is perfectly acceptable, as is plain white Xerox paper, printer paper, or inexpensive rolled paper for drafting patterns.

Seam allowances vary from pattern to pattern. Always check the instructions for the correct seam allowance and whether or not it has been included in the pattern, or must be added as you go along. Generally in quilting, the seam allowance is ¼" (6mm). If it varies from that in these projects—and it does, particularly when it comes to attaching bindings—I will let you know.

HANDLING FABRIC

I try to purchase all my fabrics for quilting at a shop that specializes in quilting fabrics. Usually that means all the fabrics they stock will be 100 percent cotton and of a similar, if not identical, weight and weave. They will also require similar care. I have used other fabrics from time to time, not always with the best results. A quilt I made for my

sister early in my quilting career was a good example of why you should use similar fabrics: one of the fabrics I used in the quilt was of a looser weave and the stress at the seams pulled it apart at the seam lines.

For cutting strips and other straight-edged pieces, I use a rotary cutter on a protective mat with transparent quilting rulers. A rotary cutter greatly increases the speed with which the pieces can be cut out. The easiest way to cut strips is to fold the fabric in half lengthwise two times, making a strip about 11 inches (28cm) wide. Then, with the top and bottom folds exactly equidistant, square off the end of the fabric, and measure and cut strips, taking care not to shift the folded fabric midcut. Applying nonskid plastic or pieces of sandpaper to the bottom of the ruler helps to prevent the fabric from slipping while you cut.

If a particular fabric is to be used for borders or binding strips as well as for piecing, I recommend that you cut out the larger pieces first and set them aside until needed. It is frustrating to finish cutting out all the little pieces only to realize that you didn't leave a large enough area for the bigger ones. By the same token, I always suggest that you purchase a bit more fabric than is strictly necessary. You never know when you may cut out a piece backwards and won't have enough extra to do it over. Believe me, it happens—especially late at night.

CHOOSING THREAD

Traditionally, white was the color of choice in thread for piecing and quilting. Today there are myriad options available. I still favor white thread for most piecing. If working with predominately dark fabrics I will switch to gray or black thread. When machine quilting I try to match the top and bobbin threads to the colors of the quilt top and backing. If there is a great variety of colors in the quilt top, I sometimes choose a nylon monofilament thread that is almost invisible. If you choose the nylon thread, use a high-quality brand in a .004 weight. It should stretch a bit, but you should be able to break it without much effort. If it does not break, it may be stronger than your fabric, which will inevitably result in tearing along the seams of your quilt.

The quilts in this book were sewn with a variety of threads for special effects. On the Pinwheels quilt (page 68), a silver holographic thread was used to indicate the swirling winds. Snowy Day (page 74) uses sparkling white thread in the satin stitching to highlight the edges of each snowflake.

These types of threads, and to a lesser extent, the regular rayon machine embroidery threads, present their own difficulties when used. Tensions need to be adjusted and sometimes bobbin threads need to be changed. I have no magic solutions for these problems, merely a list of possibilities that seem to help. For satin stitching, the product that helps me the most is tear-away stabilizer. A layer of this behind the area being stitched usually makes the difference between flat, even stitches and a line of rippled stitches. Silicone products, such as Sewer's Aid, can be applied to the thread to help smooth its path through the needle and prevent the thread's breaking quite so frequently. Changing the weight of the bobbin thread may also help when using some of these specialty threads.

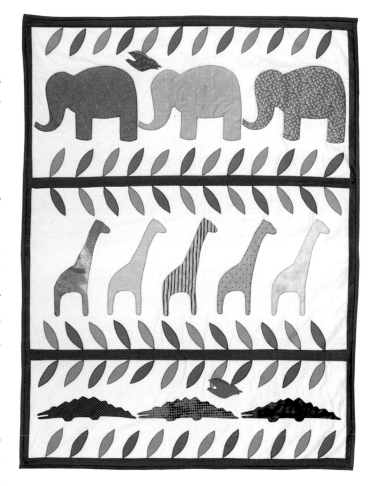

APPLIQUÉ TECHNIQUES

As you read through the directions for some of the appliquéd quilts, you will find that there are different methods for applying the appliqué pieces. The methods can be divided into three basic groups: fused appliqué, traditional needle-turn-appliqué done by hand, and machine appliqué. Fused appliqué is fast and looks nice, but it isn't recommended for a quilt that is going to get a lot of use. Fused areas are fairly stiff, especially if they are large, making it a better method for wall hangings. The traditional hand-worked appliqué is the prettiest, but the machine appliqué speeds up the assembly tremendously and looks so good that the choice between the two will come down to a matter of personal preference.

Whether you choose to work by hand or machine, there are many products available to make your work easier.

Plastic-coated freezer paper makes a great appliqué template. Ironed to the reverse of your fabric, it provides an edge against which you can fold the correct seam allowance, and it holds the appliqué in perfect shape while you are sewing it down. After the piece is stitched down, you can carefully cut away the back fabric and remove the freezer paper. Alternatively, if the shape is relatively uncomplicated, as in the Kites quilt (page 62), you can iron the seam allowances in place, then remove the paper before sewing down the appliqué. In addition to freezer paper, there's a water-soluble stabilizer available that you can use to "line" pattern pieces for sewing by machine. The Field of Flowers quilt on page 102 will provide more information on that process. Special appliqué pins that are about ½ inch (1.5cm) long are available to hold your pieces in place and won't catch your thread every other stitch. Water-soluble basting glues can be used with pins or instead of them to hold seam allowances under or to keep pieces in place for sewing.

PRESSING AND MARKING

Pressing is one step of the assembly process that is not indicated in the directions each time it is required. Whenever you complete a step in the piecing process or sew a seam, press the finished piece and check that it is still square and matches the dimensions required. Sometimes edges need to be trimmed or seam lines need re-marking. Appliqué work (aside from that requiring fusible adhesive) generally does not get pressed, as pressing will flatten the work, eliminating the wonderful feeling of dimension you've just created. A light steam can remove most wrinkles, but if you really feel you need to press the piece, do so with the piece face down on a terry cloth towel.

When you finally have that quilt top done, it's time to give it a final pressing (unless it's appliqué work) and, if there is more to be done than just echo quilting, mark it for

quilting. There are an infinite number of marking tools available today, each with its own pluses and minuses. I have been reading lately about the drawbacks of disappearing ink markers, so if you choose these, follow the manufacturer's directions to the letter. As with all marking tools, test the one you choose on the materials you will be using. See if it washes out completely, and make sure it is visible under your sewing machine light. When I am using a template to mark my quilt top, I use a rolling chalk marker. When I'm using a ruler, I use Berol Verithin Pencils. Lately I've been particularly enamored of a mechanical pencil with a 0.7mm lead made especially for fabrics. Because the lead is so fine, the point is always sharp.

CHOOSING A BATTING

Throughout this book I have noted in the material listings the type of batting used in each particular quilt. Cotton battings tend to shift less during quilting, but many cotton battings require quilting lines quite close together. In making the quilts for this book, I have used two different cotton batts, Poly-Fil Cotton Classic and Fairfield Soft Touch Cotton Batting. The Soft Touch is much like a lightweight blanket and fairly easy to handle for that reason. It also does not require quilting in close rows. In polyester I used Mountain Mist Quilt-Light Batting, Poly-Fil Traditional Batting, and Poly-Fil Low-Loft Batting. My favorite in this group is the Mountain Mist Quilt-Light for the drapability in the finished quilt. In the end, I advise you to try several types to see what works best for you.

BASTING

There are two ways you can hold the layers together for quilting: either by basting or by using safety pins. With the old-fashioned basting method, you sew long stitches back and forth across the quilt, dividing it into approximately 4-inch (10cm) squares. With the safety pin method, secure safety pins between the quilting lines, dividing the piece roughly into areas of the same size. Safety pins are much faster but do have some drawbacks. For one, they leave holes in the fabric (which, truthfully, do tend to disappear), and for another, they hurt your fingers.

When you baste the layers together, particularly if you are working with white or light-colored fabrics, take care that there are no dark-colored scraps of thread or fabric stuck between the top layer and the batting. They will show through, making at least a disturbing shadow on the surface of the quilt.

MACHINE QUILTING

Because of the pressure of looming deadlines, all the quilts in this book were quilted by machine. Of course any of them may be quilted by hand if that is what you desire. If you have not done much machine quilting, you may not know the pleasures of working with a walking foot. Nowadays one can be fitted to nearly every make and model of sewing machine (see Sources on page 116). After using one, you will never again want to machine-quilt without it. If you are really adept with your sewing machine, you may employ free-motion machine quilting for your project, particularly on a quilt like Snowy Day (page 74). Free-motion machine quilting requires a darning foot on your machine with the feed dogs lowered. It enables you to move the quilt in any direction without stopping to turn the fabric. The method is tremendously liberating, but it takes a considerable amount of practice to master. In certain situations (around the vegetables on the American Gothic Bunnies quilt [page 34]), irregular stitches are camouflaged by the nap of the flannel, making it an acceptable alternative to traditional straight sewing.

In several of the projects you will be directed to "stitch in the ditch" when quilting. As you look at the seam line between two pieces, you will note that, depending on which way the seam allowance was ironed, one side will be higher than the other. When you stitch in the ditch, you stitch right along the lower side of the seam line and even in it, if pos-

sible. You may find it necessary to place a hand on either side of the area being worked to hold the seam open for easier stitching. When you remove the piece from the machine, the higher side of the seam will rise up again, ever so slightly, hiding the quilting stitches.

BINDING

The last area worked on any quilt is the binding strips. Some people swear by bias binding. I find it leaves awkward triangles of fabric to deal with, and it frequently requires careful handling to get it to lie flat. I prefer to cut straight strips of fabric six times the width of the desired binding plus ¼ inch (6mm). A ½-inch (1.5cm) binding, for example, would require a 3¼-inch (8cm)-wide strip. This strip is then folded in half lengthwise and, with raw edges even, sewn to the right side of the quilt. When you trim your batting and backing, make sure you leave a seam allowance the same width as the desired binding. That batting and backing will fill the binding strips, leaving them soft and plump like the rest of the quilt.

CREATURE

CHAPTER TWO

FEATURES

JUNGLE CONGA LINE

✤ SIZE: 36" × 48" (91 × 122CM)

In an animal conga line, elephants, giraffes, and alligators march across this quilt on panels separated by stylized greenery. Bright pink birds flutter down here and there to see what's happening.

materials

- ✽ **4" × 12" (10 × 30cm) pieces of each of three green prints**
- ✽ **8" × 12" (20 × 30cm) pieces of each of five gold prints**
- ✽ **10" × 12" (25 × 30cm) pieces of each of three gray prints**
- ✽ **¼ yd (23cm) each of medium green and dark green solids**
- ✽ **½ yd (46cm) brown**
- ✽ **1½ yd (1.5m) each of unbleached muslin and backing fabric**
- ✽ **Scraps of two different bright pink fabrics**
- ✽ **3 yds (2.8m) of paper-backed fusible adhesive**
- ✽ **Batting (Poly-Fil Cotton Classic)**
- ✽ **Rayon machine embroidery thread, black**
- ✽ **Matching threads**
- ✽ **Template material**

From muslin, cut three strips, 11" × 36" (28 × 91cm), 16¾" × 36" (43 × 91cm) and 17¾" × 36" (45 × 91cm). Enlarge and transfer animal patterns from pages 21–23 to template material and cut out. On paper backing of fusible adhesive trace elephant and alligator three times each; giraffe five times. Cut the shapes apart. Following manufacturer's directions, fuse the adhesive elephants to wrong side of grays, alligators to wrong side of greens, and giraffes to wrong side of gold print fabrics. Cut out on marked lines.

Centering animals top to bottom and side to side, arrange giraffes on widest muslin strip, elephants on medium-wide strip, and alligators on narrowest strip. Following manufacturer's directions, peel off paper backing and fuse in place. Machine blanket stitch with black rayon machine embroidery thread around outside edges of each animal appliqué.

From brown fabric, piecing as necessary, cut four sashing strips each 1⅝" × 36" (4 × 91cm); two inner side borders, each 1¼" × 48" (3 × 122cm); and four binding strips, two 1¼" × 36½" (3 × 93cm) and two 1¼" × 48" (3 × 122cm). Set inner side borders and binding strips aside. Stitch one sashing strip to each long side of elephant and alligator panels. Sew giraffe panel between the two, with elephants on top and alligators on the bottom.

Trace leaf pattern on next page seventy-two times to paper backing of fusible web. Cut group in half and fuse thirty-six to each shade of solid green fabrics. Cut out on marked lines. Alternating shades of green, fuse twelve leaves evenly spaced along each side of sashing strips. Work machine blanket stitch around each leaf, as for animals. Trace bird and back wing patterns twice to paper backing of fusible web. Fuse to back of pink scraps and cut out. Position as desired, overlapping leaves on elephant and alligator panels. Fuse in place, taking care that main piece of bird overlaps bottom edge of back wing. Work machine blanket stitch around as before. Sew inner side borders to each long side of quilt top.

Lay backing fabric face down on flat surface. Smooth batting over backing. Center quilt top on batting and backing. Baste layers together. With machine threaded on top with off-white or invisible nylon thread, quilt around each animal and along either edge of sashing strips and inside side borders. If desired, quilt around each leaf as well. Trim batting and backing even with quilt top. Having right sides together and raw edges even, and using a ¼" (6mm) seam, sew long binding strips to long sides of quilt. Folding under ¼" (6mm), turn excess fabric to the back and slipstitch folded edge just over seam line. Folding in ¼" (6mm) on each end of remaining binding strips sew, in the same manner, to top and bottom of quilt.

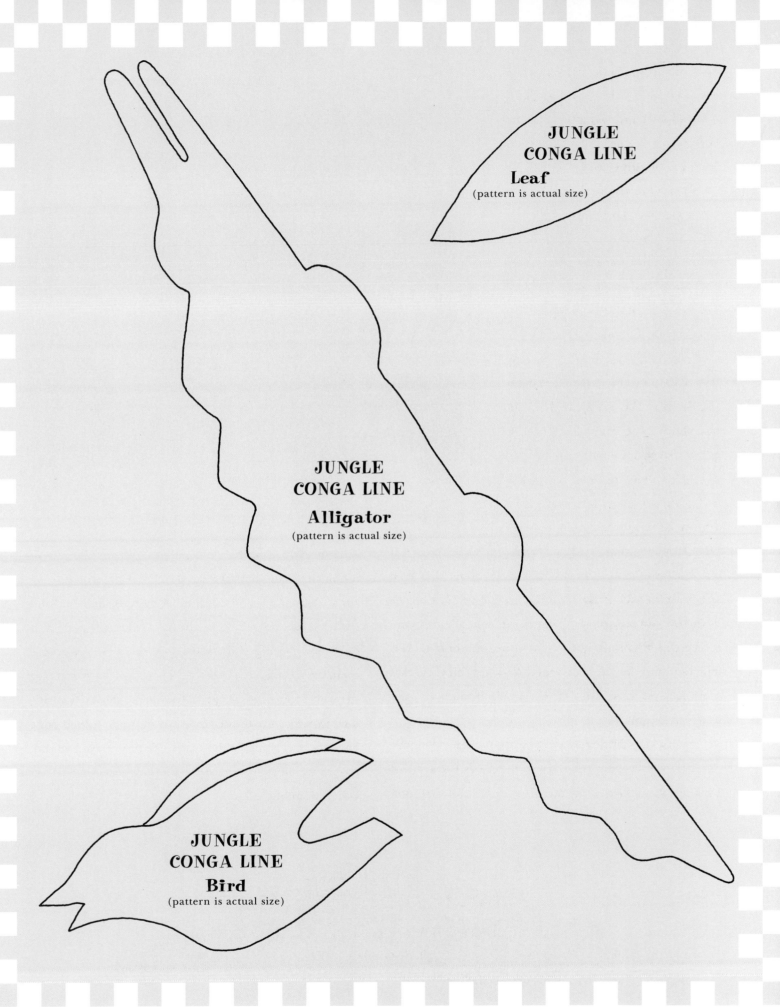

JUNGLE CONGA LINE

Leaf

(pattern is actual size)

JUNGLE CONGA LINE

Alligator

(pattern is actual size)

JUNGLE CONGA LINE

Bird

(pattern is actual size)

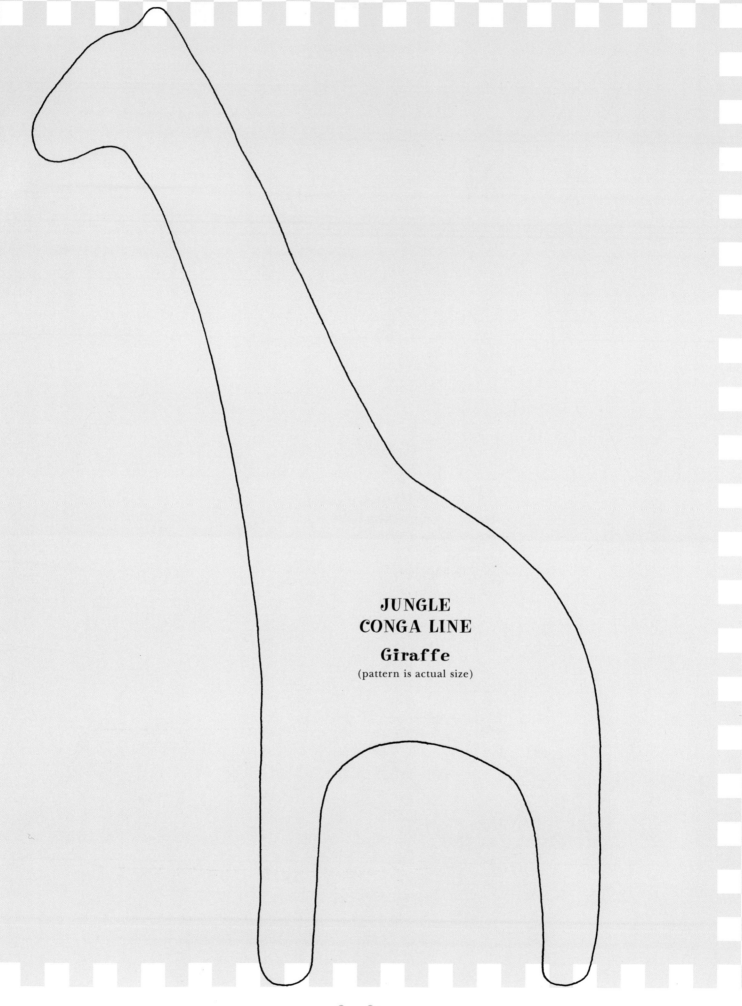

**JUNGLE
CONGA LINE**

Giraffe

(pattern is actual size)

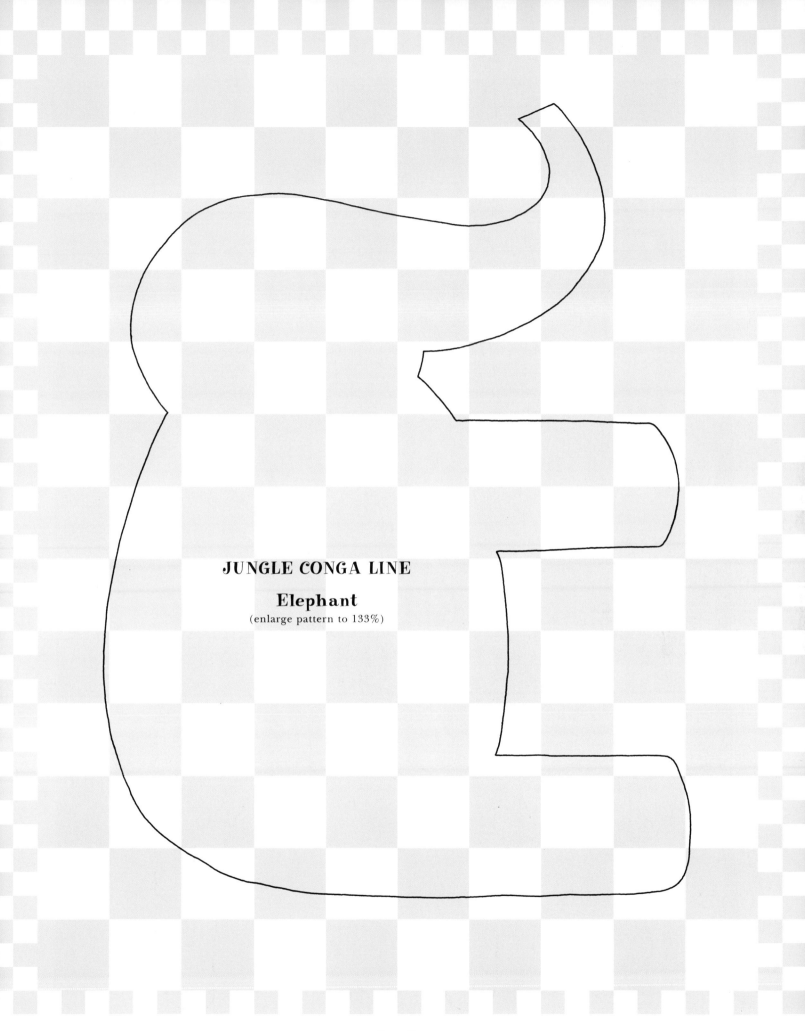

JUNGLE CONGA LINE

Elephant
(enlarge pattern to 133%)

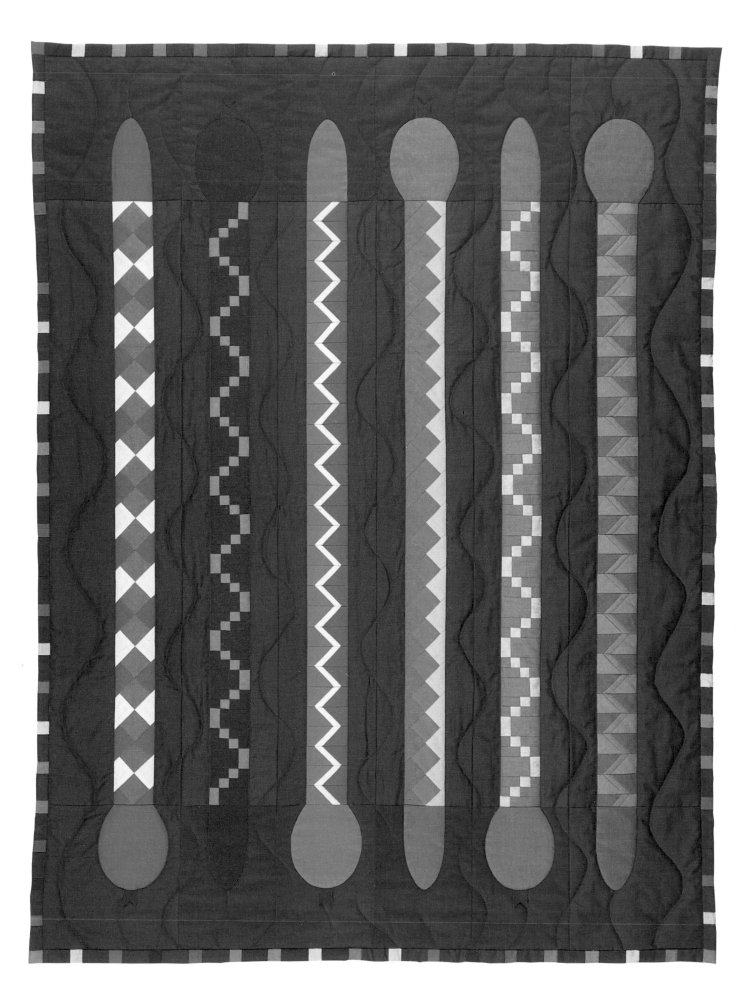

CREATURE FEATURES

SEMINOLE SNAKES

*Signaling friendly intent with their outrageous color patterns,
these snakes, assembled in strips using Seminole piecing techniques,
will slither their way right into your heart.*

materials

- **2½ yds (2.5m) of dark blue fabric (for front and backing)**
- **¼ yd (23cm) pieces of fabric in assorted colors (I used dark and light salmon, pink, neon green, kelly green, teal, fuchsia, dark and light orange, turquoise, light yellow-green, dark yellow, and lavender. If you really like a particular color and would like to use it in more than one snake, purchase ½ yd [46cm] of it.)**
- **Scrap of bright red**
- **Scrap of fusible adhesive**
- **Batting (Mountain Mist Quilt-Light)**
- **White and dark blue thread**
- **See-through ruler with 45 degree marking**
- **Chalk marking pencil**

The Seminole piecing technique used to make this quilt is really much easier than it appears. Strips are cut from several colors and sewn together. Then these strips are cut into pieces and reassembled to create the colorful patterns. Accurate seaming and cutting are the most important factors in achieving the striking effects.

The snakes are made from three different patterns, each pattern being used twice with different color combinations to create six different snakes.

Diamond pattern: For diamonds, cut a strip 1⅝" (4cm) wide by the width of the fabric (44/45" [112/114cm]) and a strip of each outer color 2¼" (5.5cm) by the width of the fabric. Stitch one outer strip to either side of diamond (narrower) strip. Press seams to outside. Cut assembled strip into 1⅝" (4cm) segments, cutting square across the seams. Reassemble the pieces on the diagonal, matching the bottom of one diamond section to the top of the next. Press seams to one side. Where you put the outside colors determines which patterned snake you will be creating. If you put all the same color on one side you will have the pattern shown on the orange and turquoise snake; if you alternate the colors, the effect will resemble the teal and orange snake. (See finished quilt on the opposite page for reference.)

Zigzag pattern: Of each outer color, cut two strips 1½" (4cm) by the width of the fabric (44/45" [112/114cm]). Of the center color, cut two strips ¾" (2cm) by the width of the fabric. Assemble two strips each with one outer color on one side of center strip, and the other color on the opposite side. Press seams away from center strip. Fold strip in half, taking care to line up the seams, and use ruler with angle markings to cut on a 45-degree angle into 1½" (4cm) pieces. This will produce a set of mirror-image pieces, which when rejoined create the zigzag effect. Join the pieces by lining up the center strip. As with the diamond pattern above, joining the pieces with the same outer color all on one side or alternating will create two different effects.

Stepping Stone pattern: Of main color cut one strip each, 1", 1½", and 2" (2.5, 4, and 5cm) by the width of the

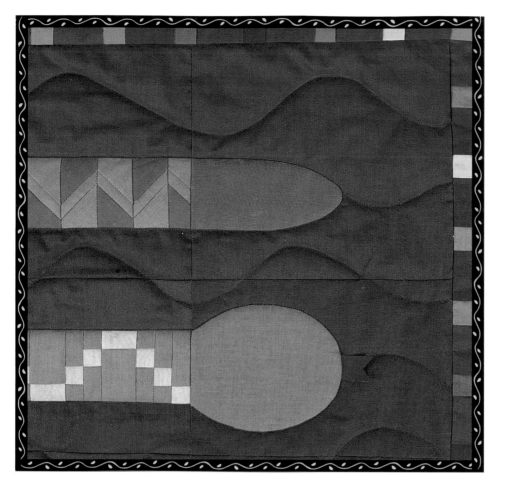

and tails for each snake from matching fabrics. Press seam allowances to wrong sides. From red fabric cut two approximately 2" × 6" (5 × 15cm) pieces, and with fusible adhesive, fuse the two pieces together. Using tongue pattern, cut six tongues from fused red fabric.

Decide on and make a note or diagram of the arrangement of the snakes. Sew one 2" (5cm) strip to either side of four middle snake bodies. To remaining bodies, sew one 2" (5cm) strip to the inner side of each and one 4" (10cm) strip to each outer edge. Trim each snake to 31" (79cm) long. With raw edges even and right sides together, pin head or tail with seam allowances pressed under and then one blue backing piece (5½" × 8¼" [14 × 21cm]) to body of each middle snake. Sew in place. For the two outside snakes use backing squares (7½" × 8¼" [19 × 21cm]). Take care that you are attaching the heads and tails to the correct ends of body according to your arrangement. Press heads/tails and backing squares away from bodies and hand appliqué in place to backing. When stitching heads down, first position tongues under heads and stitch securely by machine before appliquéing head in place over tongue. This will ensure that the tongue will not be easily pulled out by inquisitive fingers. Sew assembled snakes together, taking care to follow your arrangement and have heads and tails at alternating ends of quilt top. Press.

Lay backing out flat, right side down. Smooth batting on top of backing. Center quilt top, right side up, onto batting and backing. Baste layers together. Using matching threads, stitch in the ditch (see page 15) around each snake, lifting tongues as you go and stitching underneath them. With chalk or other marking tool, lightly sketch a

fabric (44/45" [112/114cm]). Of contrasting color, cut two strips each 1" (2.5cm) by the width of the fabric. Sew one contrasting strip to one side of 2" (5cm) color strip. Sew remaining main color strips to each side of remaining contrasting color strip. Press seams away from contrasting color strip. Cut the two-piece strip into 1½" (4cm) pieces cutting square across the seams. Cut the remaining (three-piece) strip into 1" (2.5cm) pieces. Reassemble the pieces to create a staircase effect as shown in the fuchsia and green snakes.

After pressing seams, lay completed strips out and carefully trim each to 2½" (6cm) wide, centering pattern in that area. From dark blue, cut a 36" × 48" (91 × 122cm) piece for backing and ten strips each 2" × 32" (5 × 81cm); two strips each 4" × 32"(10 × 81cm); eight 5½" × 8¼" (14 × 21cm) pieces; and four 7½" × 8¼" (19 × 21cm) pieces. From remaining fabric, cut eight 1⅞" × 26" (4.5 × 66cm) strips, piecing if necessary.

Using head and tail patterns on next page and adding ¼" (6mm) seam allowance on sides and bottoms, cut heads

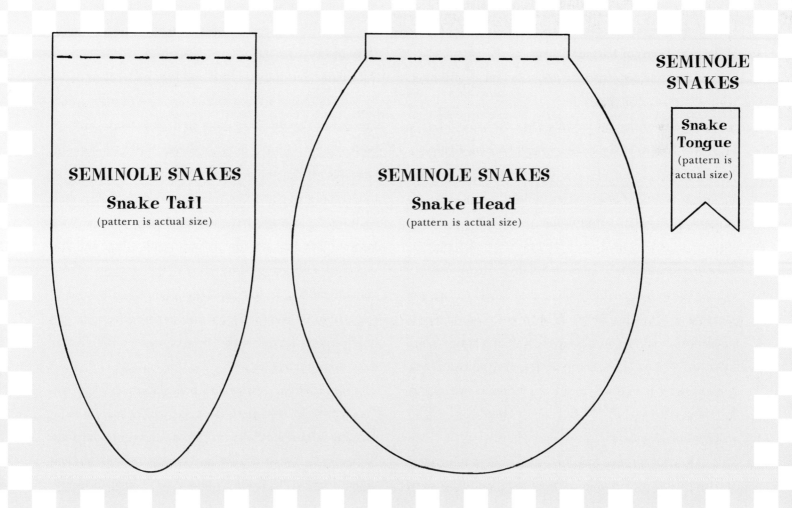

wavy line down the center of the space between each snake, alongside the outer snakes and from head/tail to edge on either end. Quilt along marked lines. Trim batting and backing to ½" (1.5cm) beyond top.

Cut a ⅞" × 26" (2.2 × 66cm) strip from each of the eight remaining colors. Sew color strips alternating with remaining blue strips. Press seams to one side. Cut assembled piece into 2" (5cm) strips. Join strips to make one long piece of binding. In order to make the binding fit perfectly on each edge a little maneuvering will be necessary. First measure binding against each short edge, cutting it slightly longer if necessary, so that these strips end with

whole blue pieces. Turn binding strip over. To take up any excess length, make each seam between blue and color strips just a tiny bit deeper. Do this on each edge until strip fits well. No one will ever notice that some pieces may be a tiny bit smaller than others. Repeat this process on longer sides, but this time, end each strip with a whole colored piece. Mark a ¼" (6mm) seam allowance on wrong side of binding strip. Match raw edge of binding strip with raw edge of quilt top, right sides together, and stitch along marked line. Repeat on each edge. Fold binding to back and turning under ¼" (6mm) on raw edges, slipstitch just over binding seam line.

SEMINOLE SNAKES

Snake Tongue
(pattern is actual size)

SEMINOLE SNAKES

Snake Tail
(pattern is actual size)

SEMINOLE SNAKES

Snake Head
(pattern is actual size)

PAPAGALLO

✦ ✦ ✦ SIZE: 36" × 48" (91 × 122CM)

Brilliant with exotic, tropical colors and boasting a wing of three-dimensional "feathers," this South American parrot quilt evokes the colorful mola appliqué work of the Kuna Indians.

materials

- 1½ yds (1.5m) of neon green fabric
- 1 yd (1m) of black fabric
- ½ yd (46cm) of purple print
- ½ yd (46cm) of green fabric
- ¼ yd (23cm) of orange fabric
- Assorted pieces of colorful prints and solids including several oranges
- 1½ yds (1.5m) of backing fabric
- Assorted threads in bright colors as well as matching portions of bird's body
- Nylon monofilament thread
- 2½ yds (2.5m) of lightweight paper-backed, fusible adhesive
- 2½ yds (2.5m) of tear-away stabilizer
- Batting (Poly-Fil Cotton Classic)

From neon green fabric, cut four binding strips 3¼" (8cm) wide by the length of the fabric and set aside. Cut center panel 20" × 31" (51 × 79cm) of neon green fabric. From purple print, cut two border strips 1½" × 22½" (4 × 57cm) and two 1½" × 31" (4 × 79cm). Sew longer strips to long sides of center panel and sew shorter strips across top and bottom of center panel. Press seams to outside.

From black fabric, cut two outer border strips 7½" × 33½" (19 × 85cm) and two 7½" × 36" (19 × 91cm). Sew shorter strips to either side of center panel, longer strips across top and bottom, again pressing seams to the outside.

Enlarge and trace eighteen large and eighteen small triangles from page 31 to paper backing of fusible adhesive and cut out close to line. Follow manufacturer's directions to fuse triangles to wrong side of assorted print and solid fabrics. Cut out on marked lines. Arrange randomly around black border, fusing large pieces in place first, then a smaller piece in the center of each large piece.

Enlarge and transfer bird and foot patterns to paper backing of fusible adhesive and trim close to cutting line. Fuse bird to green fabric, foot to orange fabric, and cut both out on cutting lines. Position bird and foot on assembled background piece having body overlap top of foot and fuse in place. Cut tear-away stabilizer larger than each fused piece and baste or pin to back of work. With machine set on medium to wide satin stitch and top threaded with contrasting thread for triangle pieces, matching thread for bird and foot, satin stitch around all edges of fused pieces, taking care to cover the edge well or it will come up under the stress of usage. Carefully tear away excess stabilizer.

From assorted orange and print fabrics cut approximately fifty 3½" (9cm) squares. Fold in half, right sides together and sew ¼" (6mm) from edge opposite fold. Roll seam to center of piece and finger-press sides. Using pencil and having feather pattern ¼" (6mm) from one

end, mark for curved shaping. Stitch along marked line, trim corners, and turn right side out. Press.

Enlarge and transfer wing pattern from next page to orange fabric, including both placement and stitching lines. Cut out with generous allowance around larger shape. Arrange and pin feathers on larger shape, starting the first row with ends touching placement line and succeeding rows overlapping the previous row by approximately 2" (5cm), working up to and over top of wing. Uppermost rows will hang off top of wing. Using a narrow zigzag stitch, sew feathers to wing across top raw edges.

Using stitching line only, trace a second wing pattern to orange fabric for wing lining. Cut out ¼" (6mm) from stitching line. Matching stitching lines, pin lining on top of feathered wing piece and stitch on marked lines, taking care to catch in tops of feathers on upper few rows, and not to catch in those on lower few rows (pin them up and out of the way). Leave an opening along one side for turning. Trim edges. Turn wing right side out and slipstitch opening closed. Position wing on bird and pin in place. With machine set on medium zigzag, and top threaded with monofilament, carefully stitch wing in place along all edges, keeping feathers free on sides and bottom.

Trace eye pattern within body pattern on page 33 to paper backing of fusible adhesive and cut out close to lines. Fuse to back of desired fabrics and cut out on marked lines. Fuse eye in position on bird. With machine set on medium zigzag and top threaded with matching threads, satin stitch over fused edges. Transfer markings for decorative stitching onto bird. Alternating red and orange threads, work satin stitch spokes radiating from eye. Work orange beak line, narrowing the satin stitch from widest at head to about half as wide at tip of beak. Work alternating orange and red lines of satin stitch on tail, widening the stitch as you work from body to tip of tail.

Press assembled top, taking care not to damage stitching with a too hot iron. Center panel will be quilted with a stipple pattern. If you feel more comfortable having a line to follow, mark it now, using a pencil or chalk marker to sketch random curving lines filling areas devoid of appliqué work.

Lay backing out flat with right side down. Smooth batting over backing. Center quilt top right side up on batting and backing. Baste layers together. With matching threads or invisible nylon thread, stitch in the ditch (see page 15) around bird and wing. Stipple-quilt open areas of center panel. Stitch in the ditch around inside and outside of purple border and around each appliquéd triangle. Trim batting and backing even with quilt top.

With wrong sides together, fold binding strips in half lengthwise. With raw edges even, and excess binding extending evenly at either end, sew strips to right side of quilt using a ½" (1.5cm) seam. Miter corners. Turn folded edge of binding to back and slipstitch in place over seam line.

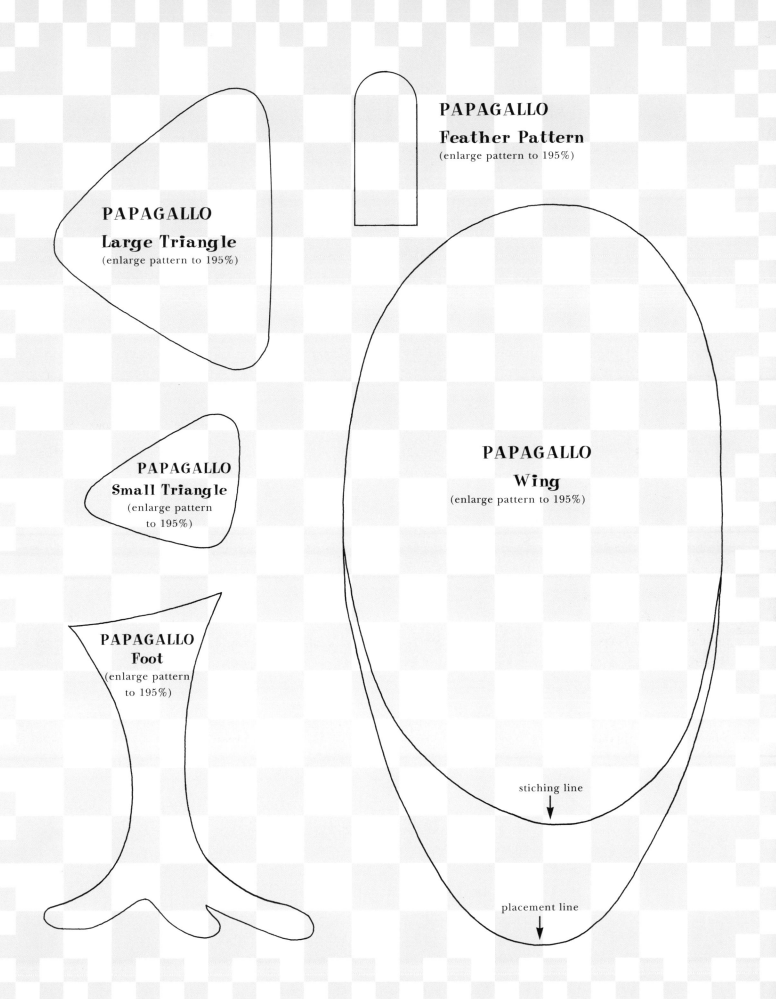

PAPAGALLO

Feather Pattern

(enlarge pattern to 195%)

PAPAGALLO

Large Triangle

(enlarge pattern to 195%)

PAPAGALLO

Small Triangle

(enlarge pattern
to 195%)

PAPAGALLO

Foot

(enlarge pattern
to 195%)

PAPAGALLO

Wing

(enlarge pattern to 195%)

stiching line

placement line

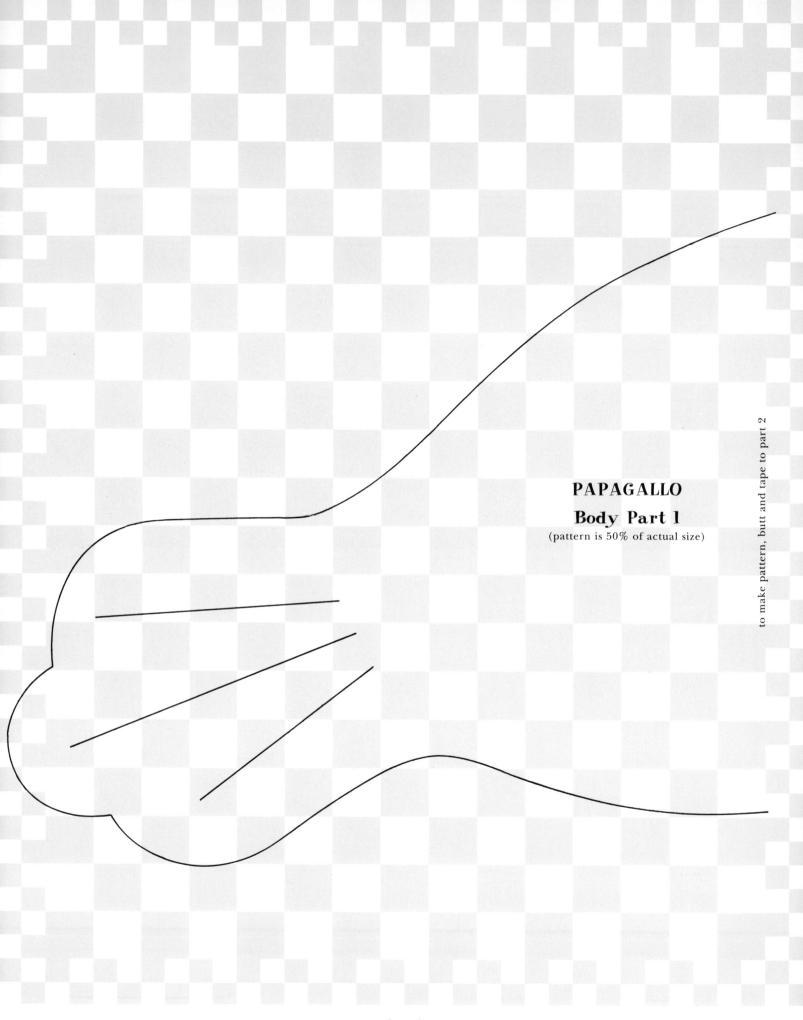

PAPAGALLO

Body Part 1

(pattern is 50% of actual size)

to make pattern, butt and tape to part 2

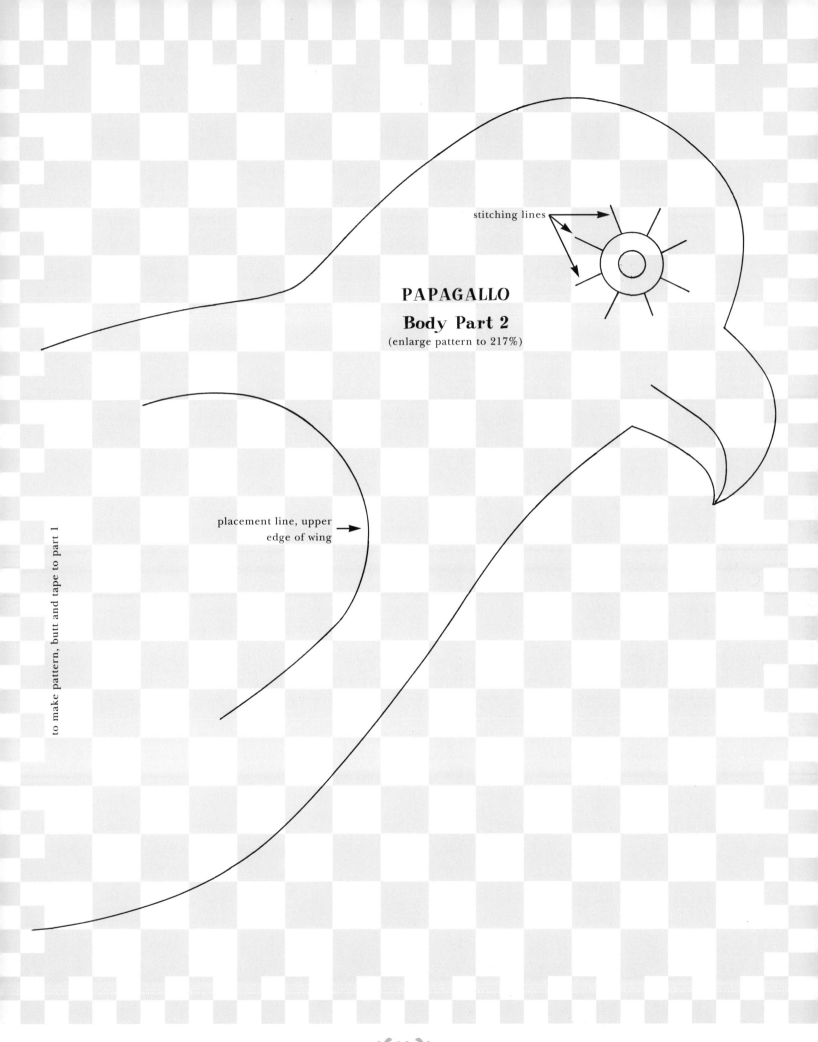

stitching lines

PAPAGALLO
Body Part 2
(enlarge pattern to 217%)

placement line, upper
edge of wing

to make pattern, butt and tape to part 1

AMERICAN GOTHIC BUNNIES

✦ ✦ ✦ SIZE: 36½" × 49½" (93 × 126CM)

*A humorous rendition of the classic painting, these two farmers
are rabbits appliquéd in fuzzy white flannel. The "fruit" of their efforts
is hand-painted onto the flannel borders around them.*

materials

- ⊞ **3 yds (2.8m) of good quality white flannel (includes backing)**
- ⊞ **1 yd (1m) of orange tone on tone print**
- ⊞ **¼ yd (23cm) of blue tone on tone print**
- ⊞ **¼ yd (23cm) of green vegetable print**
- ⊞ **½ yd (46cm) of white fabric**
- ⊞ **Scraps of light green, brown print, pink, light brown, light blue, and gray fabric**
- ⊞ **Matching threads**
- ⊞ **Embroidery floss, dark gray and gold**
- ⊞ **Fabric paints, green yellow, orange, and red**
- ⊞ **Fabric marker, black**
- ⊞ **Pencil for use on fabric (I prefer a mechanical pencil with thin, fine lead.)**
- ⊞ **Paintbrushes**
- ⊞ **Scrap paper**
- ⊞ **Batting (Fairfield Soft Touch Cotton)**

Cut four pieces of scrap paper, two 8½" × 32" (22 × 81cm) and two 8½" × 35½" (22 × 90cm). Tape the strips together with longer strips across top and bottom, shorter strips as sides to make border template. Arrange vegetable patterns on pages 37–38, five per border strip, centered top to bottom and side to side.

You can flop motifs and alter leaves as desired for best effect. You can also extend motifs across seams from one strip to another as I have done. When you are satisfied with the arrangement, mark outlines with a black marker. Cut strips apart again.

From flannel, cut or tear two strips 11" × 34" (28 × 86cm) and two 11" × 38" (28 × 96cm). Center one flannel strip over each paper strip. With pencil, trace outlines of vegetables onto flannel. Before beginning to paint borders, test a painting technique on scraps of flannel. What worked best for me was to use a very thin paint applied with a nearly dry brush. Keep folded paper towels next to your work area and after dipping your brush into the paint, dab it onto the paper towel until rapid bleeding slows. Then apply paint to the fabric with light brushing strokes. Be sure to let each color dry thoroughly before going on to the next color. When paint is dry, go over the outlines of the vegetables with a black fabric marker, again using a stroking motion and feeling free to waver. Go outside the lines and generally make it look very loose and free-form. For vegetables that extend onto another panel, work the outlining after final assembly of quilt top. Heat, set finished painting,

if necessary, following manufacturer's directions. Set border pieces aside.

Cut a piece of flannel approximately 40" × 53" (102 × 135cm) for backing and set this aside.

For the method of appliqué used here, you will need to cut a pattern for each piece to be applied. Trace patterns lightly with a pencil onto fabric. Cut pieces out ⅛"–¼" (3–6mm) beyond the traced line for edges that will be turned under and ½"–¾" (1.5–2cm) for edges that will be overlapped. Pin the pieces in place on the background. With a fine needle and matching thread, turn under about ½" (1.5cm) at a time along marked line and sew in place with small invisible stitches. Invisible stitches are achieved by taking a small bit of background fabric onto the needle then coming back to the front through the fold of the piece being applied and pulling the needle through. Begin the next stitch by going into the background fabric again directly behind the place where you emerged from the fold. Continue in same manner along all edges to be appliquéd. Refer to the photograph on page 35 and the lines transferred onto each piece for applying successive pieces.

With basting stitches or fabric pencil, mark a rectangle 20" × 33½" (51 × 85cm) on orange tone on tone fabric for background. Enlarge bunny patterns on page 39 to tracing or other lightweight paper. Cut out individual pieces, labeling them if desired. Trace both bunny heads onto flannel. Trace and cut inner ears and noses from pink and apply to heads. Cut out bunny heads and pin heads in place, centered within marked area of orange background fabric. Appliqué all exposed edges in place; baste down edges that will later be overlapped. When both heads have been applied, cut out from flannel and apply

the feet of both bunnies, and male bunny's left arm and right upper arm.

Trace the female bunny's skirt to the green vegetable print, then trace and cut out basket from brown print and apply to skirt before cutting out skirt. Apply skirt to background, overlapping feet. Apply female bunny's arms, traced and cut from flannel, taking care that the hands fall into place over the basket handle. Trace and cut bodice from light green fabric and sew in place, covering the top of the skirt and arms. Trace and cut male bunny's overalls from blue tonal fabric and stitch in place. Trace and cut cuffs from light blue and apply. Trace and cut fork handle and fork from light brown and gray fabrics respectively and apply. Lastly, appliqué bunny's right hand in place over the fork handle.

Transfer eye and mouth markings to faces and with dark gray embroidery floss, satin stitch the eyes and outline or stem stitch the mouth. Appliqué a small button shape, cut from scraps of gold fabric, to shoulders of bunny overalls. With gold floss, work overall fasteners from shoulder strap to button and back again. Lightly transfer overall details (waistline, pockets) to overalls. These will later be used as quilting lines.

Using markings as a guide, center bunnies and trim appliqué panel to 20" × 32½" (51 × 83cm). Trim painted borders to 9" × 32½" (23 × 83cm) for side strips and 9" × 36½" (23 × 93cm) for top and bottom strips. Using ¼" (6mm) seams, sew side strips then top and bottom strips to center panel. At this point, finish painting and outlining any vegetables that extend onto neighboring panels.

Lay backing fabric right side down onto flat surface. Smooth batting over backing. Center quilt top right side up onto batting and backing. Baste layers together. With white thread in bobbin and matching thread (or nylon thread) in top, quilt around bunnies, and along outside edges of clothing including the markings transferred to overalls and lines delineating "toes" on feet. Quilt around pitchfork. Quilt around each vegetable on border panels. I found it easiest to put a darning foot on the machine, lower the feed dogs, and quilt around the vegetables using free-motion quilting. Uneven stitches will be well hidden in the nap of the flannel. Trim batting and backing to be even with borders.

From white solid fabric, cut five strips, 3¼" (8cm) wide by the width of the fabric (44/45" [112/114cm]). Fold one strip in half lengthwise and having cut edges even, stitch to short edge of quilt front using a ¼" (6mm) seam. Turn folded edge to back and slipstitch just over seam line. Repeat along bottom edge with second strip. Cut and join remaining three strips on the bias. Use pieced binding strip to bind the remaining edges, turning under ½" (1.5cm) at each corner for a neat finish.

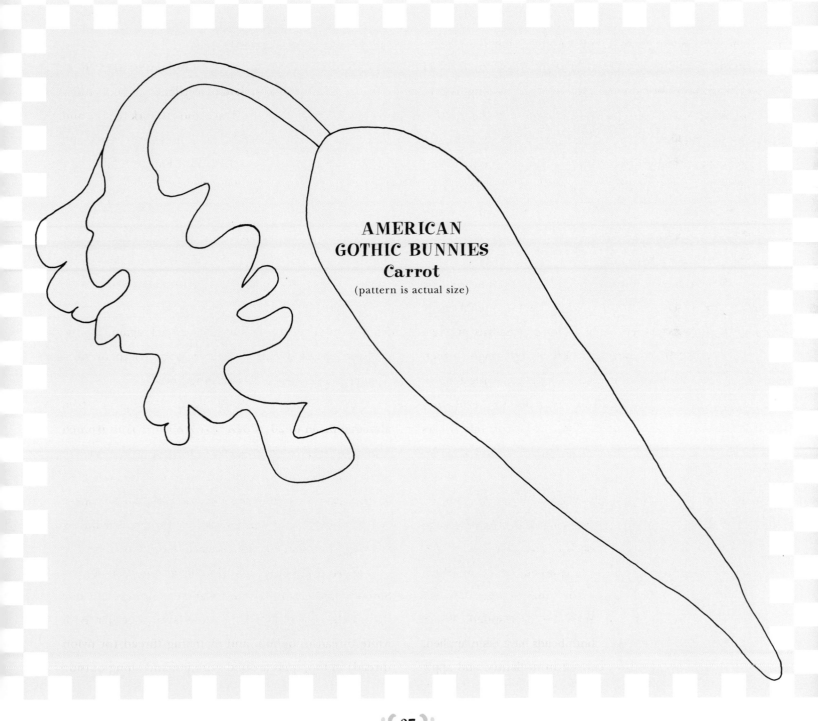

AMERICAN GOTHIC BUNNIES
Carrot
(pattern is actual size)

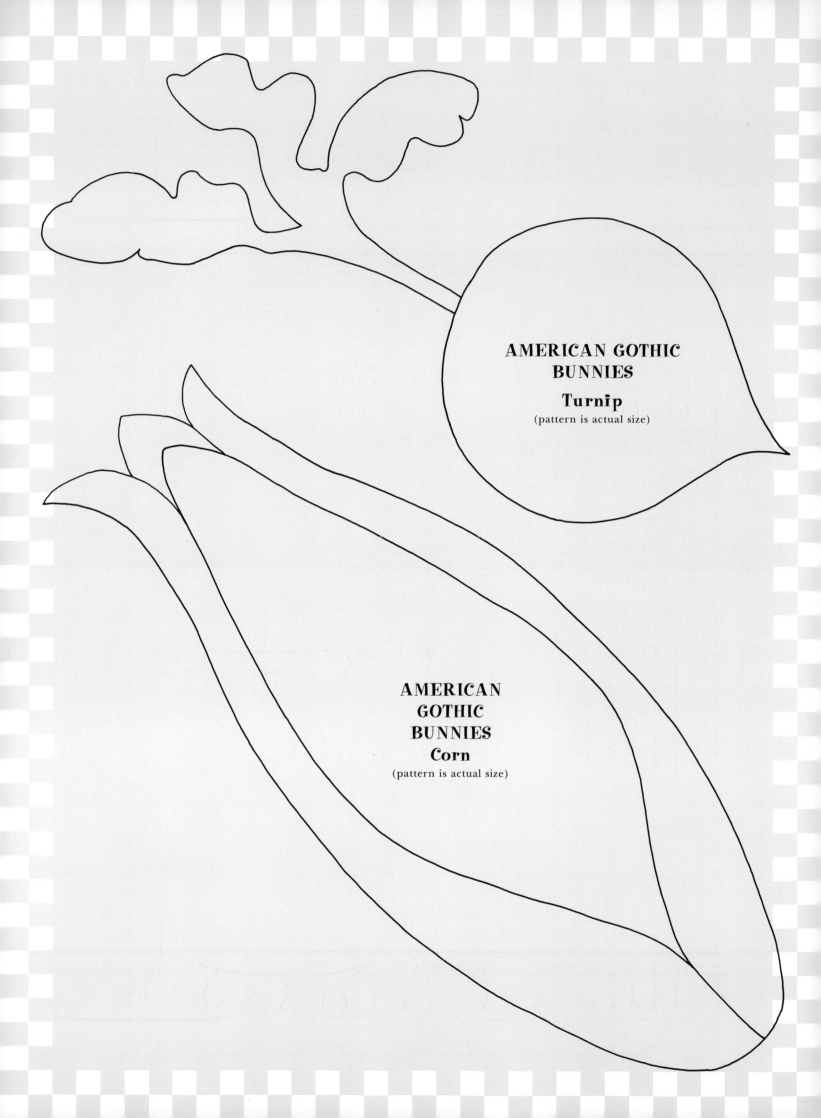

AMERICAN GOTHIC
BUNNIES
Turnip
(pattern is actual size)

AMERICAN
GOTHIC
BUNNIES
Corn
(pattern is actual size)

AMERICAN GOTHIC BUNNIES

Bunnies

(enlarge to 315%
male bunny
should be
31½" [80cm] tall
at full size.)

VROOM,

CHAPTER THREE

VROOM

TRAFFIC JAM

Cars, trucks, and buses, all headed off in different directions on their very important errands, make for one extremely colorful traffic jam on this quilt.

m a t e r i a l s

- ◼ 1½ yds (1.5m) of white fabric
- ◼ 1 yd (1m) of black fabric
- ◼ ¾ yd (69cm) of yellow fabric
- ◼ ½ yd (46cm) of gray fabric
- ◼ Assorted ¼ yd (23cm) cuts of several fabrics (I used 8 different colors.)
- ◼ 1½ yds (1.5m) of backing fabric
- ◼ 3 yds (3m) of paper lightweight backed fusible adhesive
- ◼ 2½ yds (2.5m) of tear-away stabilizer
- ◼ Batting (Fairfield Soft Touch Cotton)
- ◼ Black and white thread

From white fabric, cut two pieces, each 12½" by 24½" (32 × 62cm) for bus backgrounds; three pieces, each 12½" × 16½" (32 × 42cm) for truck backgrounds; and five pieces, each 8½" × 11½" (21.5 × 29cm) for car backgrounds. Cut a matching set of pieces from tear-away stabilizer. From yellow fabric, cut five strips each 2½" × 24" (6.5 × 61cm). From black fabric, cut five strips each 1½" × 24" (4 × 61cm). Using ¼" (6mm) seams, sew black and yellow strips together alternately. Set aside.

Enlarge patterns on pages 45–47 and transfer to paper backing of fusible adhesive as follows: two bus bodies and bus stripes; four bus wheels and hubcaps; eight large bus windows; two small bus windows and two front bus windows; three truck bodies and cabs; six truck wheels and hubcaps; three regular and three front windows; five car bodies; five each front, middle, and back windows; and ten car tires and hubcaps. Cut pieces apart and fuse to their respective fabrics following manufacturer's directions. Cut out each shape along marked lines. Center bodies of buses, according to layouts, on bus background pieces and fuse in place according to manufacturer's directions. Place windows, tires, hubcaps, and stripes in position and fuse in place.

Position truck cab and body on truck background according to pattern on page 43, with a slight overlap between the two, and fuse in place. Position windows, wheels, and hubcaps, also fusing in place. Position car bodies on car backgrounds, according to layouts, and fuse in place. Position and fuse windows, wheels, and hubcaps.

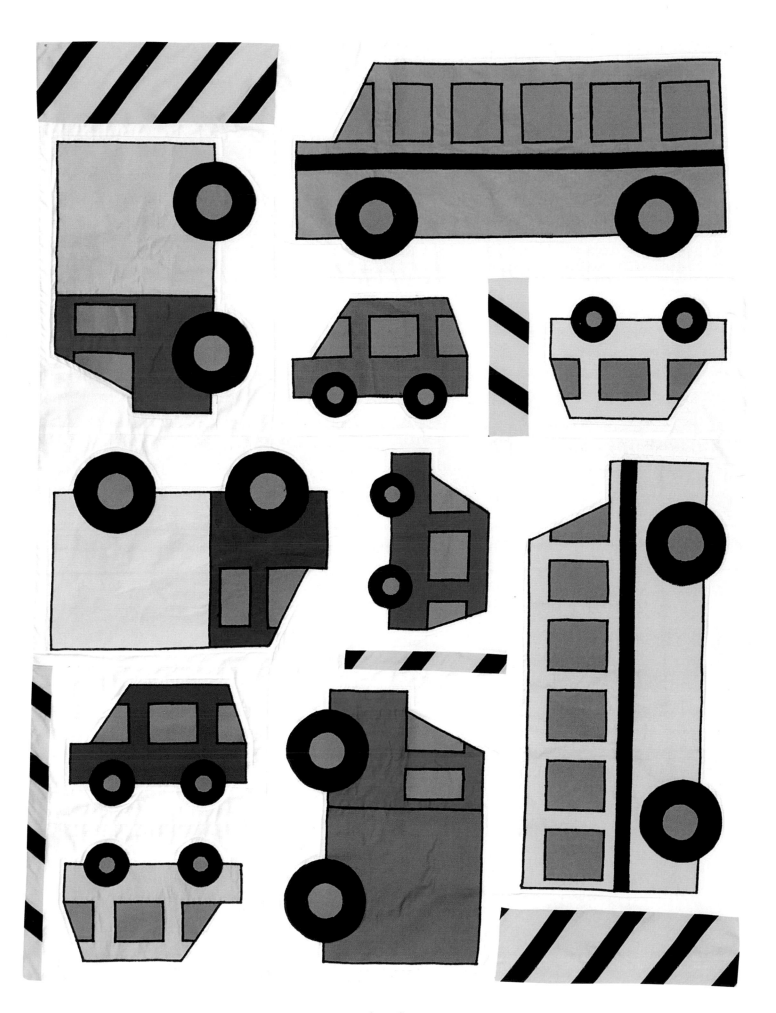

Assembly Diagram

Pin matching piece of stabilizer to back of each assembled piece. With sewing machine set on medium-width zigzag and threaded with black thread, satin stitch around each piece of each vehicle, taking care that the bulk of the stitching rests on the fused piece in order to hold the edges down more securely.

Mark the bias on the pieced yellow and black strip and cut the following: two pieces each 4½" × 12½" (11.5 × 32cm) (A); one piece each 1½" × 8½" (4 × 21.5cm) (B); 1½" × 1½" (4 × 4cm) (C); and 2½" × 8½" (6.5 × 21.5cm) (D). Referring to above assembly diagram as necessary, sew striped piece

D between two car blocks and sew this strip to one bus block. Sew one striped piece A to end of one truck block and sew this piece to assembled car/bus piece. Sew striped piece B to one end of car block, then sew this piece to one short end of a truck piece. Sew two remaining car blocks together along one long edge. Sew striped piece C to one long edge of this assembled car block. Sew remaining long edge of assembled car block to long edge of remaining truck block. Sew this three-vehicle piece to the previously assembled two-vehicle piece along long sides. Sew last remaining striped piece to end of last bus block and then sew that piece to the truck/car assembly just created.

Lay backing fabric right side down on flat surface. Smooth batting over backing. Center quilt top, right side up, onto batting and backing. Baste layers together. Using presser foot as guide, quilt ¼" (6mm) outside each vehicle. Trim batting and backing to ¼" (6mm) beyond quilt top. From remaining black fabric, cut binding strips, two 3¼" × 40" (8.5 × 102cm) and two 3¼" × 52" (8.5 × 132cm), piecing as necessary to achieve the length needed. With wrong sides together, fold strips in half lengthwise. Using a ½" (1.5cm) seam, sew to quilt front having raw edges even and leaving at least 1" (2.5cm) excess at each end. Miter the corners and turn folded edge to back, slipstitching in place just over seam line.

Alternatively, this quilt could be easily adapted to and would hold up to heavy usage better if rendered in patchwork. By adding a few lines to each pattern, window areas in particular, piecing could be simplified. I would still appliqué the wheels, but without using the fusible adhesive.

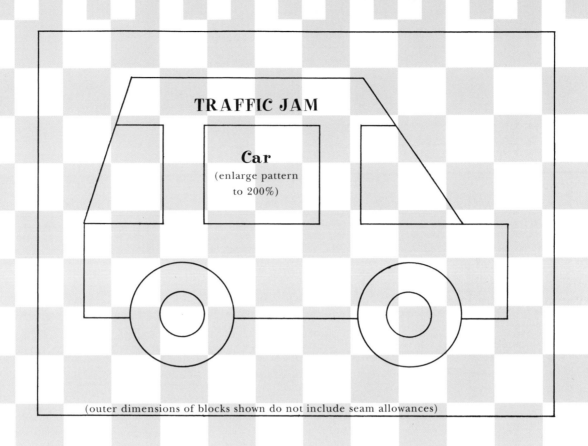

TRAFFIC JAM

Car
(enlarge pattern
to 200%)

(outer dimensions of blocks shown do not include seam allowances)

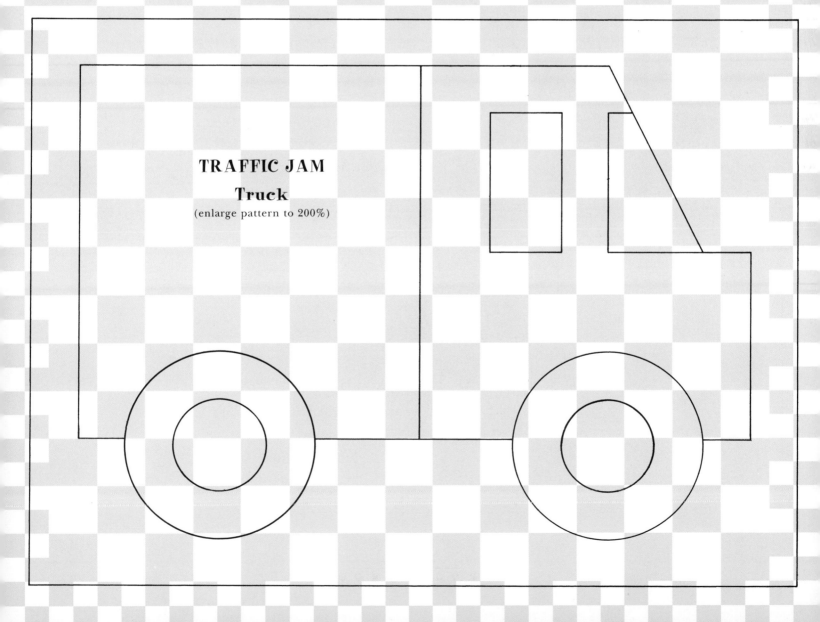

TRAFFIC JAM

Truck
(enlarge pattern to 200%)

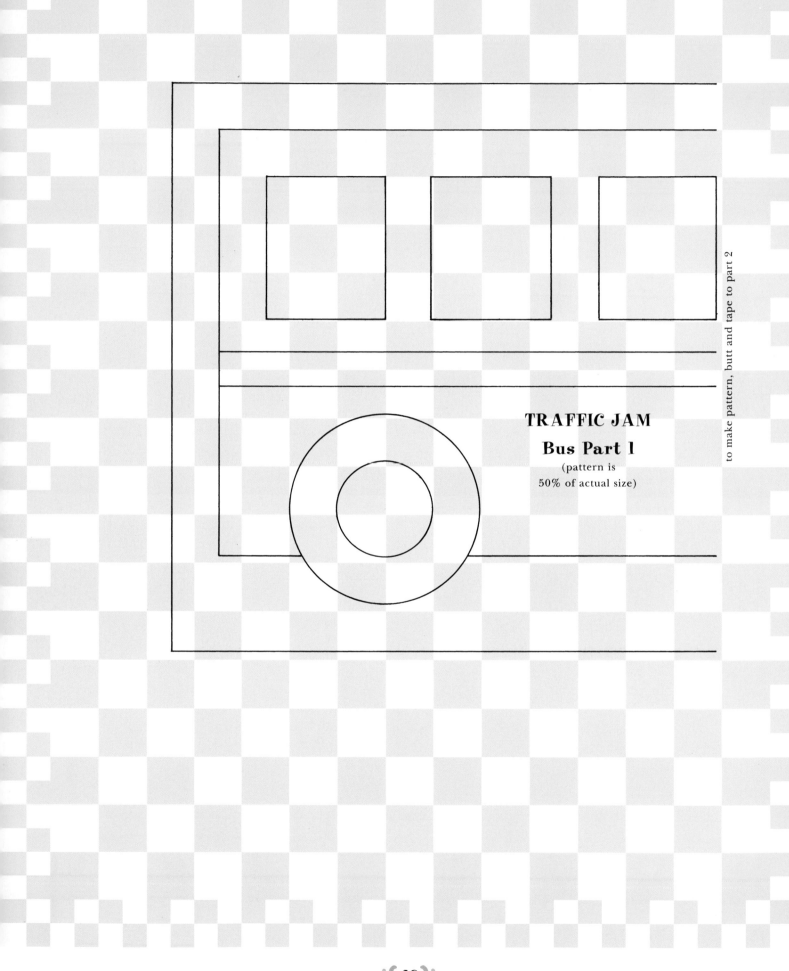

TRAFFIC JAM

Bus Part 1

(pattern is
50% of actual size)

to make pattern, butt and tape to part 2

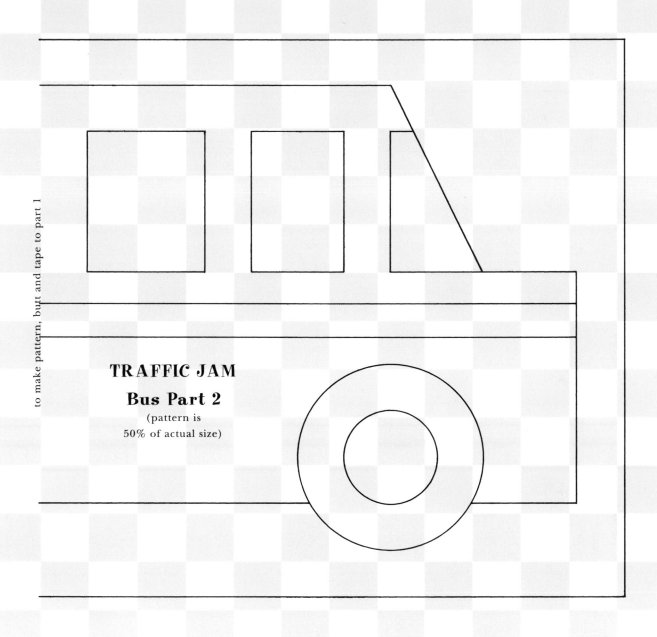

to make pattern, butt and tape to part 1

TRAFFIC JAM

Bus Part 2

(pattern is
50% of actual size)

It must be something about flying free as a bird, way up high in the sky,
that makes kids love airplanes. Against skies with puffy clouds, these crayon-bright
airplanes will send many a miniaviator into rapture.

m a t e r i a l s

- ✖ **2 yds (2m) of sky with clouds print**
- ✖ **¼ yd (23cm) of each red, green, and yellow fabric**
- ✖ **Scraps of gray and medium blue fabric**
- ✖ **1½ yd (1.5m) of backing fabric**
- ✖ **Matching threads**
- ✖ **Batting (Mountain Mist Quilt-Light)**
- ✖ **Template material**

Enlarge pattern on page 51 and transfer to template material adding ¼" (6mm) seam allowance all around. From sky fabric, cut four binding strips, two 3" × 28½" (7.5 × 72cm) and two 3" × 40½" (7.5 × 103cm). From remaining sky fabric and following the pattern, cut background pieces as follows: twenty-four each of A, B, D, and E pieces and twelve C pieces. Use scraps to make corner pieces, which are not labeled on general pattern.

From red, green, and yellow fabrics, cut four each of F, G, H, and J pieces. From gray fabric, cut twenty-four K pieces. Begin assembling airplanes in sections. Sew a K piece to either angled side of C piece to form rectangular propeller unit. Sew sky scrap across angled corners of each F piece. Press and trim edges square with edges of F piece. Sew one B piece to each short side of assembled F piece to form plane front unit. Sew propeller unit to top of plane front unit. Sew one A piece to each side of plane front/propeller units.

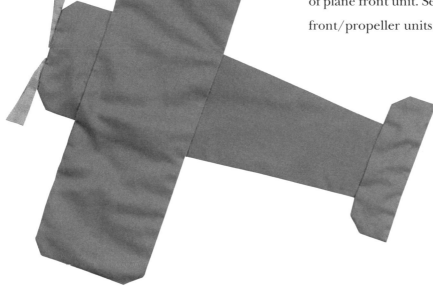

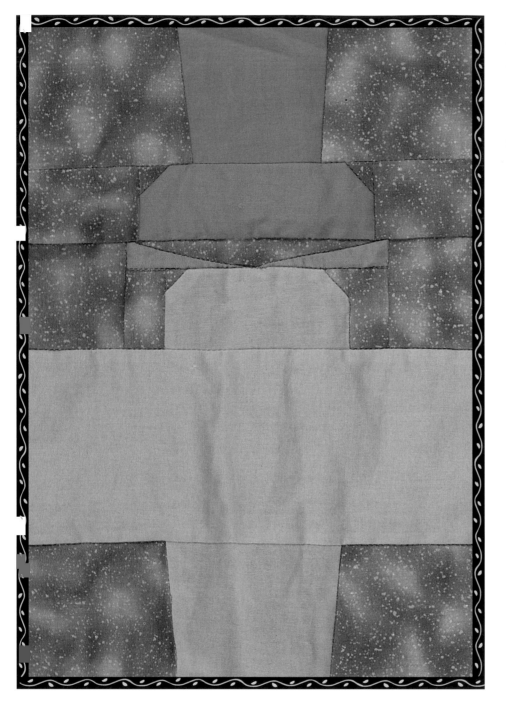

Sew assembled front/propeller units to wing units, then to plane back units, then to tail units to complete square. Refer to original diagram on page 51 as necessary for correct placement of pieces.

Sew assembled squares together, arranging planes in rows facing in opposite directions or as desired. Lay backing fabric right side down on flat surface. Smooth batting over backing. Center quilt top, right side up, onto batting and backing. Baste layers together. With thread to match backing in bobbin and thread to match top or nylon monofilament in top of machine, quilt along edges of each plane and across wing seams, if desired. Trim edges of batting and backing to ½" (1.5cm) beyond quilt top edges.

From medium blue fabric, cut eight pieces each 3" × 5½" (7.5 × 14cm) and sew one to each end of previously cut sky fabric binding strips. With right sides together pin shorter strips to top and bottom of quilt, centering sky portion of binding strip along edge. Using ¾" (2cm) seams, sew strips in place. Trim ends of strip even with quilt and fold excess to back turning under ¾" (2cm). Slipstitch folded edge just over seam line. Repeat centering and sewing process with remaining strips and side edges of quilt, this time folding under excess at ends of strips to make clean corners.

Sew sky fabric scraps to each angled corner of G piece. Press and trim edges square to form wing units. Sew one D piece to each side of each H piece, to form rectangular plane back units. Sew sky scraps to each angled corner of each J piece, pressing and trimming scraps square to form tail piece. Sew one E piece to each short end of each assembled tail piece to form tail units.

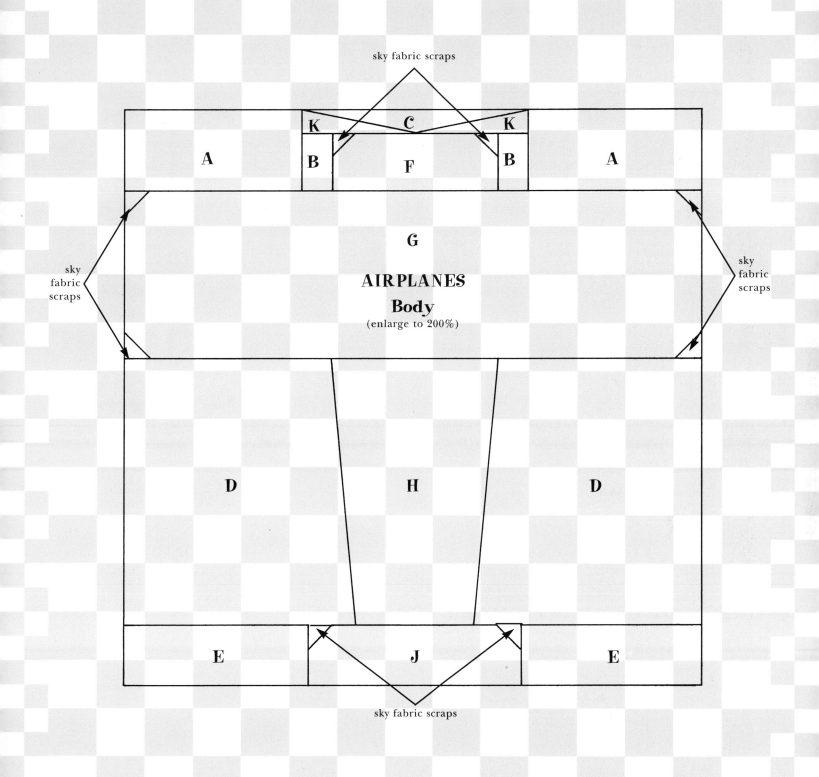

I, ROBOT

✦ ✦ ✦ SIZE: 34½" × 47½" (87 × 121CM)

A variety of gray prints and bright colors makes this
icon of tomorrow enchanting to all who find robots alluring.

materials

- 1¼ yds (1m) of neon green tone on tone print
- 1½ yds (46cm) each of dark purple print and matching purple solid fabric
- ¼ yd (23cm) of bright turquoise tone on tone print
- Assorted gray prints and bright colors (both solids and prints) with one piece of gray being at least 10" × 12" (25 × 30cm) for largest body piece
- 1½ yds (1.5m) of gray fabric for backing and binding
- Batting (Poly-Fil Low Loft)
- Large piece of graph paper
- Freezer paper (plastic coated)
- ¼ yd (23cm) tear-away stabilizer
- Matching threads and black
- Appliqué pins (optional)

Note: Borders of the pattern included here have been adjusted to eliminate the small pieces on the side borders seen in the photograph on page 53.

From neon green tone on tone fabric, cut a center panel approximately 24" × 36" (61 × 91cm), and cut 24 strips, each 1" × 7½" (2.5 × 19cm) for border and set aside. Enlarge robot master pattern on page 55 to graph paper. Trace each piece of robot to matte side of freezer paper, taking care to indicate edges that will be overlapped by other pieces. Cut out freezer paper patterns on marked lines. With a dry iron set on cotton, iron all large pattern pieces, except gauges, to the backs of their respective fabrics. Cut ⅛"–¼" (3–6mm) beyond edges to be appliquéd, ½"–¾" (1.5–2cm) beyond edges to be overlapped. Finger-press, then iron edges to be appliquéd under. When working with multiple layers of appliqué, always start with the layers farthest back and work forward. In this case, the neck, dome, and antenna would be applied before the head, and so on. Details, like facial features and gauges, are worked last.

Using master pattern to position, center first few pieces on neon green center panel. Appliqué folded edges and baste down raw edges that will be overlapped by successive layers at a later time. Continue to apply pieces until all main pieces have been appliquéd in place.

Transfer markings for gauges to fabric. Pin or tack a piece of tear-away stabilizer to back of area to be embroidered. With black thread on top and machine set on medium-width zigzag, work satin stitch details on gauges before adhering them to freezer-paper patterns and cutting out.

Smaller pattern pieces like the facial features can be worked in the same manner as large pieces. Or, mark edges of pattern pieces to front of fabric and work the needle-turn appliqué method, pinning the appliqué in place and turning under a small bit at a time with your needle as you appliqué it in place. The tiniest details can be worked in machine satin stitch or embroidery.

Trim completed robot panel to 20½" × 33" (52 × 84cm), centering robot within that space.

Enlarge and cut out border triangle pattern, adding ¼" (6mm) seam allowance all around. Fold purple solid and print fabrics in half and and using border triangle pattern, cut fourteen pair from print and ten pair from solid fabrics. Set aside half the pairs from each group. With remaining pairs of border triangles, and using ¼" (6mm) seams, sew one neon green strip to the long angled edge of each piece. Trim ends of green strips even with sides of purple pieces. Sew remaining pairs to opposite sides of green strips to form rectangles. Sew rectangles together to form border strips (two with seven print units each and two with five solid units each) with neon green fabric zigzag down the middle.

From turquoise print, cut four 7" (tkcm) squares. Transfer or trace center portion of border gauge pattern to white or light print fabric four times. With each piece backed by tear-away stabilizer, machine set for medium-width zigzag and threaded on top with black thread, work markings and arrows. Cut out ⅛"–¼" (3–6mm) beyond outside line and using needle-turn method, pin and appliqué to orange gauge backing fabric. Mark backing fabric ½" (1.5cm) beyond white edges and repeat the cutting and appliqué process, centering finished gauge on turquoise square. Trim longer border strips to 7½" × 33½" (19 × 85cm). Sew one border gauge square to each end. Center shorter border strips, one on either end of center panel, pin, and stitch in place using ¼" (6mm) seams. Trim ends even with edges of center panel. Pin longer strips to either side of panel, matching seam lines, and stitch in place.

Lay backing out right side down on flat surface. Smooth batting over backing. Center quilt top right side up on batting and backing. Baste the layers together. Quilt around all major body shapes of robot. Quilt around center panel and along seams between gauge squares and border strips. Using presser foot as guide, quilt ¼" (6mm) from all outside edges.

Trim batting to ½" (1.5cm) beyond quilt top. Trim backing to 1" (2.5cm) beyond batting. Turning under ¼" (6mm) on raw edges, fold backing to front and slipstitch in place to quilting line around outside edges of quilt.

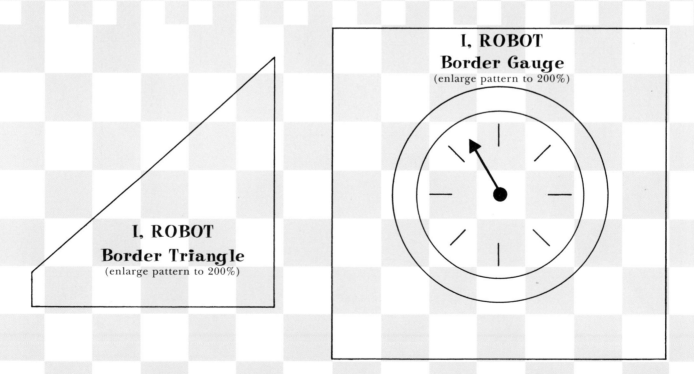

I, ROBOT
Border Triangle
(enlarge pattern to 200%)

I, ROBOT
Border Gauge
(enlarge pattern to 200%)

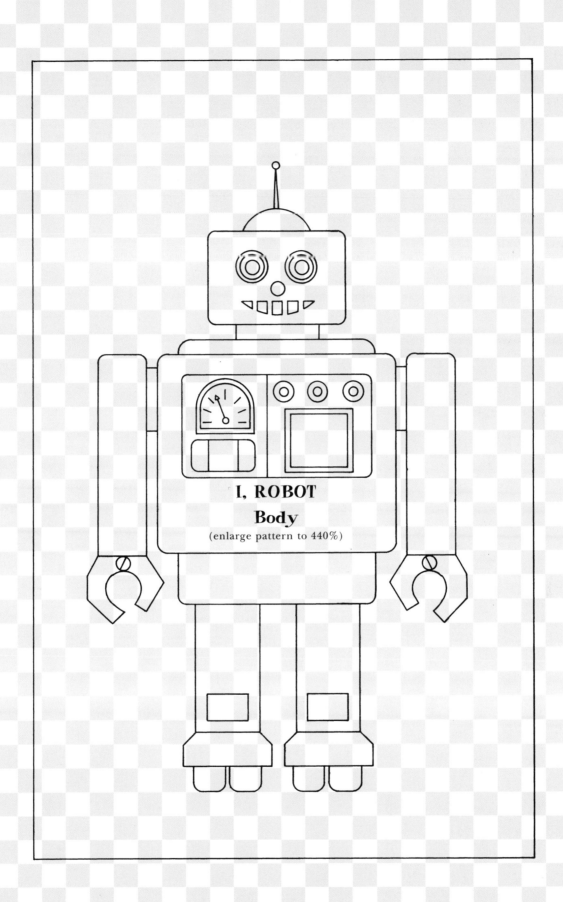

I, ROBOT

Body

(enlarge pattern to 440%)

OH THE

CHAPTER FOUR

WEATHER OUTSIDE

OUTSIDE

M I L K Y   W A Y

✤ SIZE: 38" × 50" (96.5 × 127CM)

*Rich dark blues set off the gold and white fabrics in this
traditional patchwork pattern, evoking a brilliant nighttime sky
perfect for casting wishes upon.*

m a t e r i a l s

- ¼ yd (23cm) of each of two blue prints
- 1 yd (1m) of a third blue print
- 2 yds (2m) of a fourth blue print for backing and binding
- ¼ yd (23cm) each of white and a white on off-white print
- ¼ yd (23cm) each of three different gold prints
- ½ yd (46cm) of lightweight paper-backed fusible adhesive
- ¾ yd (69cm) of tearaway stabilizer
- Batting (Poly-Fil Traditional)
- Matching threads
- Template material

On paper, draft a 3" (8cm) square and divide it in half, diagonally, from corner to corner. Trace one resulting triangle to template material adding a ¼" (6mm) seam allowance all around. Also mark out a 3" (8cm) square and a 1½" (4cm) square adding the same seam allowances. Enlarge and transfer stars and swags to template material, adding no seam allowances. Cut out templates. Trace stars and swags four times each to paper backing of fusible adhesive. Cut shapes out close to lines and fuse, according to manufacturer's directions, to back of gold fabrics, working as economically as possible. From remaining gold fabrics, cut fifty triangles and four large squares.

From white on off-white print, cut four large squares and twenty-two triangles. From white cut seventy-eight small squares. From smaller cuts of blue prints, cut seventy-eight small squares and twenty-eight triangles. From 1 yd (1m) cut of blue print, cut two strips 8" × 27½" (20 × 70cm) and two strips 8" × 30½"(20 × 77cm) for inner borders.

Using ¼" (6mm) seams, sew twenty-eight blue triangles to twenty-eight gold triangles along longest sides to form twenty-eight 3½" (9cm) squares. Sew remaining gold triangles to white triangles in the same manner. Sew small blue and white squares together in pairs. Sew two pairs together, checkerboard fashion, to make thirty-nine 3½" (9cm) squares. Referring to diagram as necessary, assemble center panel from large gold and white squares and assembled squares, sewing squares into rows then joining rows to form center panel. Sew one short blue strip to each long side

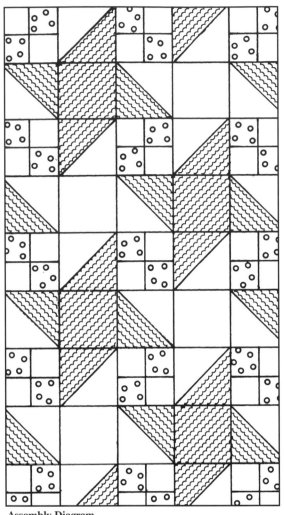

Assembly Diagram

of center panel. Sew remaining strips to each end. From remaining pieced squares, assemble outer borders, making two strips of twelve squares and two strips of seventeen squares, alternating checkerboard squares with blue/gold squares and having the gold triangles facing in one direction up to the midpoint then reversed for the remainder of the strip. Sew the longer strips to the longer edges of the quilt top, the shorter strips across the remaining edges.

Arrange stars and swags around each corner of inner borders, taking care to butt or slightly overlap swags together along center line. Fuse in place according to manufacturer's directions. Cut tear-away stabilizer into four pieces each approximately 11" × 20" (28 × 51cm) and pin one behind each set of fused pieces. With machine set on medium-width zigzag and threaded with gold thread, satin stitch around all edges of fused stars and swags, taking care to keep stitching more on the edges of fused pieces than on background. Tear away excess stabilizer.

Lay backing fabric out right side down on flat surface. Smooth batting over backing. Center quilt top, right side up, onto batting and backing. Baste layers together. With machine threaded with matching thread (or nylon) on top, quilt around pieced stars on center panel. Quilt around satin-stitched appliqués and around outside of both the center panel and inner border. If desired you may also quilt between each square unit on outer border. Lastly, quilt ¼" (6mm) from outer edges of quilt top, using presser foot as guide.

Trim batting to ¾" (2cm) beyond quilt top. Trim backing fabric to 1¼" (3cm) beyond batting. Fold backing to front, turning under ¼" (6mm) along raw edges and slipstitch to front of quilt, just over stitching line. Miter the corners as you turn them if desired.

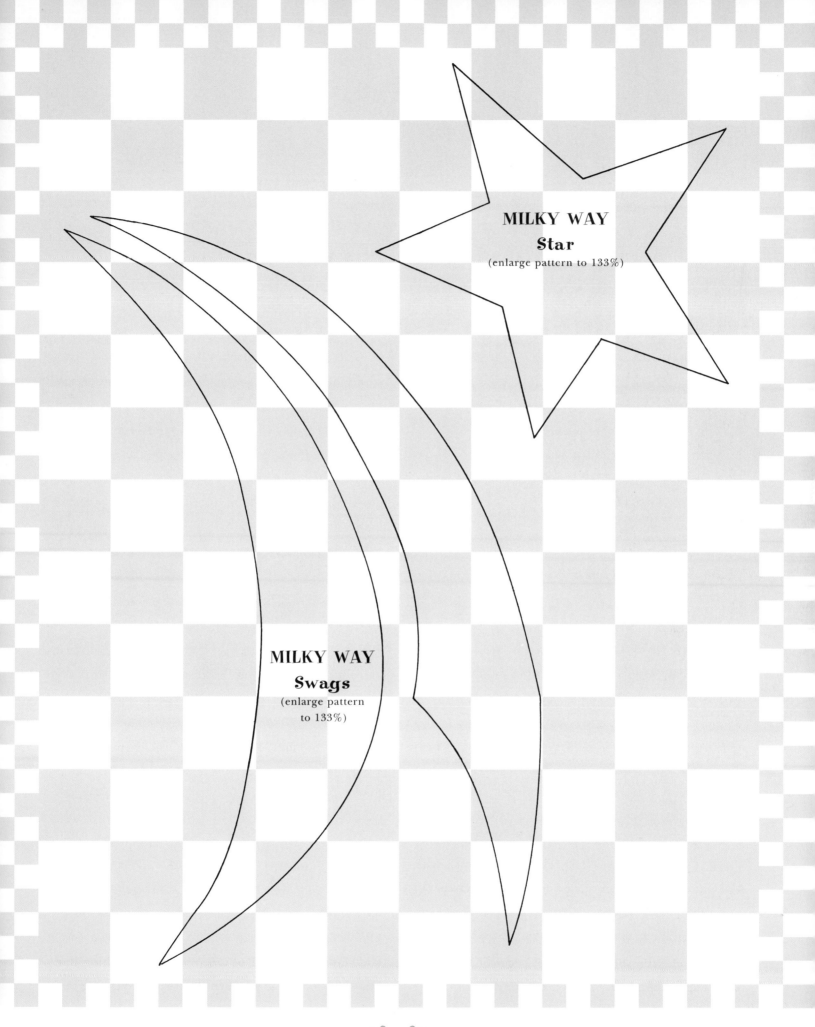

MILKY WAY
Star
(enlarge pattern to 133%)

MILKY WAY
Swags
(enlarge pattern
to 133%)

KITES

✦ ✦ Size: 36" × 48" (91 × 122cm)

On a bright, blustery day what could be better fun than
sending a kite soaring aloft. In this quilt, these cheery kites, one
with a three-dimensional tail, sail against a springtime sky.

materials

- ▓ 1½ yds (1.5m) of sky print fabric
- ▓ ¼ yd (23cm) pieces of four different green prints
- ▓ ½ yd (46cm) of bright pink print
- ▓ Scraps of yellow print and blue print
- ▓ ½ yd (46cm) each of black and light turquoise fabric
- ▓ ¼ yd (23cm) of white fabric
- ▓ 1½ yds (1.5m) backing fabric
- ▓ Batting (Poly-Fil Low Loft)
- ▓ 1½ yds (1.5m) of purple satin ribbon, 1" (2.5cm) wide
- ▓ Tracing paper
- ▓ Freezer paper, plastic coated
- ▓ Tearaway stabilizer
- ▓ Matching threads
- ▓ Nylon monofilament thread for machine quilting

Enlarge patterns for kites and ground and bushes patterns on pages 66–67 to tracing paper. Trace individual ground pieces separately to tracing paper adding ¼" (6mm) seam allowances all around and marking for placement. Cut from assorted green print fabrics. Join, following ground master pattern on page 67 and using ¼" (6mm) seams. Make individual tracings of each bush shape and cut out each piece. Trace each to selected green print fabrics and when cutting out, add ⅛"–¼" (3–6mm) allowances along upper edges and ½"–¾" (1.5–2cm) along edges that will be overlapped by the assembled earth piece.

Working with bushes farthest back first, pin bushes in place, using master pattern as a guide to bottom right hand corner of sky fabric. Using matching thread and needle-turn appliqué method (see American Gothic Bunny quilt on page 34) appliqué upper edges in place to sky fabric and basting down bottom edge. Apply the foreground bushes in the same manner. Lastly, place the assembled ground piece in position overlapping the appliquéd bushes and needle-turn appliqué it in place along upper edge. Bast remaining lower and side edges in place. With pencil, pins, or basting stitches lightly mark background for outer edges of quilt top, using ground appliqués to establish bottom and right side edges. You should mark an area approximately 33" × 45" (84 × 114cm).

Trace kite patterns to matte or dull side of freezer paper and cut out. Using dry iron on cotton setting, fuse freezer-paper patterns to wrong side of fabrics, having large kite on pink fabric, medium kite on blue fabric, and small kite on yellow fabric. Cut out ¼" (6mm) beyond edge of freezer paper and press seam allowances to wrong side along edges of freezer paper. Using photograph on the opposite page as reference, arrange kites on sky background within marked limits of quilt top. Mark kite positions with pins, then working with one at a time, remove freezer paper and pin in place along all edges. Using matching thread, appliqué in place to background.

When all kites have been sewn down, lightly mark tails and strings, extending string lines all the way off the

edges of the quilt top, as well as the tail of the largest kite. Pin pieces of stabilizer behind marked areas. With machine set on narrowest zigzag for the smallest kite string and widening progressively for each kite, the widest zigzag being reserved for the tail of the largest kite, satin stitch along all marked string lines and along kite tail lines for the smaller two kites with white thread. With yellow thread satin stitch ties on yellow kite tail, widening and narrowing the width of the stitch to give them dimension. Work ties on blue kite tail with blue thread in the same way.

Cut purple ribbon into five pieces. Pleat the center of each piece of ribbon, narrowing its width to about ½" (1.5cm), and pin pieces evenly spaced along marked line for largest kite's tail. With machine set for widest zigzag, and threaded with white thread, satin stitch along marked tail line, sewing over ribbons as you go. If desired, you may alter the width of the stitches to give some dimension to the tail. Tear away excess stabilizer. Trim quilt top to 33½" × 45½" (85 × 116cm), centering appliquéd portion as much as possible within those dimensions.

From black fabric, cut ten strips each 1½" (4cm) wide by the width of the fabric (44/45" [112/114cm]). From white fabric, cut five strips each 1¼" (3cm) wide by the width of the fabric. Using ¼" (6mm) seams, sew one black strip to either side of each white strip. Press seams away from white strips. Cut pieced strips into 1¼" (3cm) sections. Reassemble sections into five equal length strips on the diagonal, matching the seam at the bottom of one white section to the seam at the top of the next white section. The resulting strips will have a row of white diamonds running down the middle. Press strips flat. Join three of the diamond strips together, then divide in half. Trim each

of the four strips to ¼" (6mm) beyond white diamonds on one side (inner side) and ½" (1.5cm) beyond diamonds on the opposite side (outer side). On shorter diamond strips, count out thirty complete diamonds and cut ¼" (6mm) beyond each end. On longer strips count out forty-three complete diamonds and cut ½" (1.5cm) beyond each end. With right sides together, pin short diamond strips to top and bottom of quilt, having inner edge (edge trimmed to ¼" [6mm]) even with raw edges. Strip should fit exactly edge to edge with quilt top. Stitch in place using a ¼" (6mm) seam. Pin remaining diamond strips to long edges of quilt in same manner, taking care the end diamonds line up with diamonds of previously applied strips.

Mark top for quilting. Lightly pencil free-form cloud shapes on sky background fabric. If desired, mark sections of ground into stripes for a garden effect. Lay backing fabric right side down on flat surface. Smooth batting over backing. Center quilt top, right side up, onto batting and backing. Baste layers together. With machine threaded with matching thread or nylon monofilament, quilt along marked lines and along edges of kites, kite strings, kite tails, along edges of bushes and ground appliqué, and along seam lines of each individual piece making up the ground appliqué. Lastly, quilt around inside edge of diamond borders. Trim batting and backing even with quilt top (½" [1.5cm] beyond outermost points of white diamond).

From light turquoise fabric cut five binding strips each 3¼" (8cm) wide by the width of the fabric (44/45" [112/114cm]). Join three of the strips along the bias and divide the assembled strip in half. With wrong sides together, fold each strip in half lengthwise. Sew longer strips to right side of longer sides, having raw edges even and using ½" (1.5cm) seams. Turn folded edge to back and slipstitch in place over seam line. Attach remaining strips in the same manner, having at least ½" (1.5cm) excess at each end. Fold overhang to back to clean-finish corner, then turn long folded edge to back and slipstitch in place over seam line.

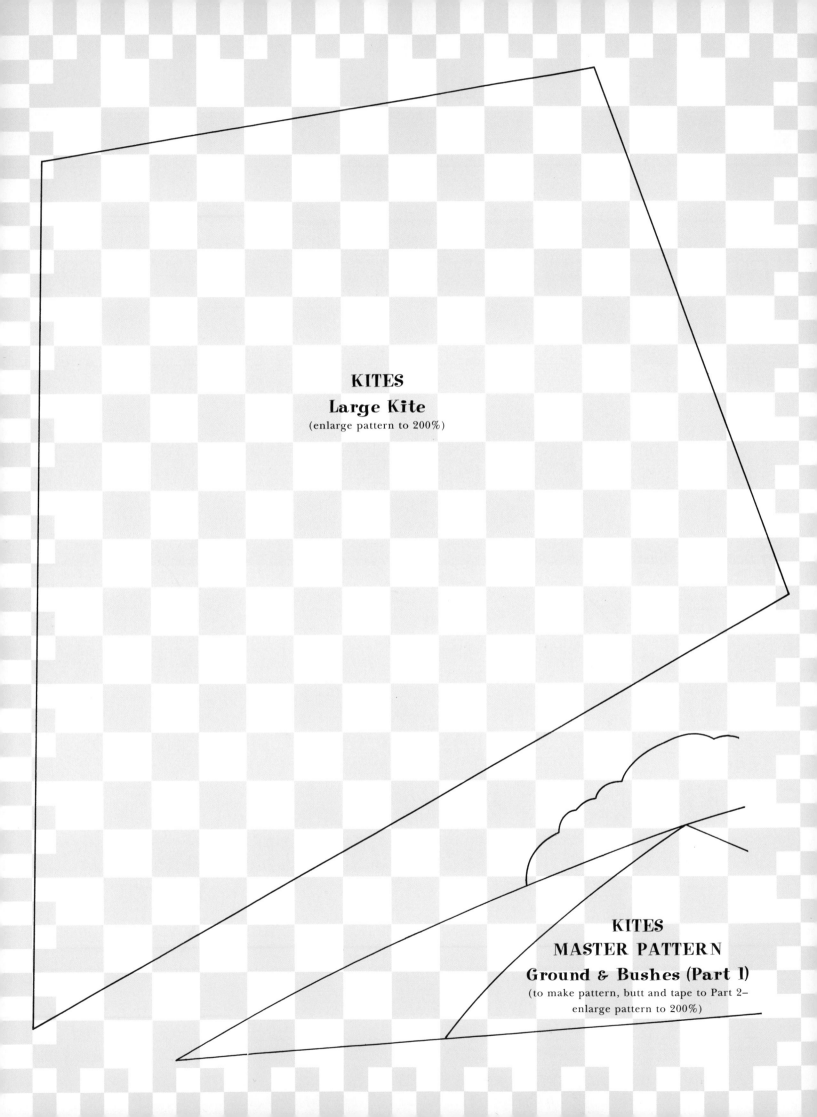

KITES
Large Kite
(enlarge pattern to 200%)

KITES
MASTER PATTERN
Ground & Bushes (Part 1)
(to make pattern, butt and tape to Part 2–
enlarge pattern to 200%)

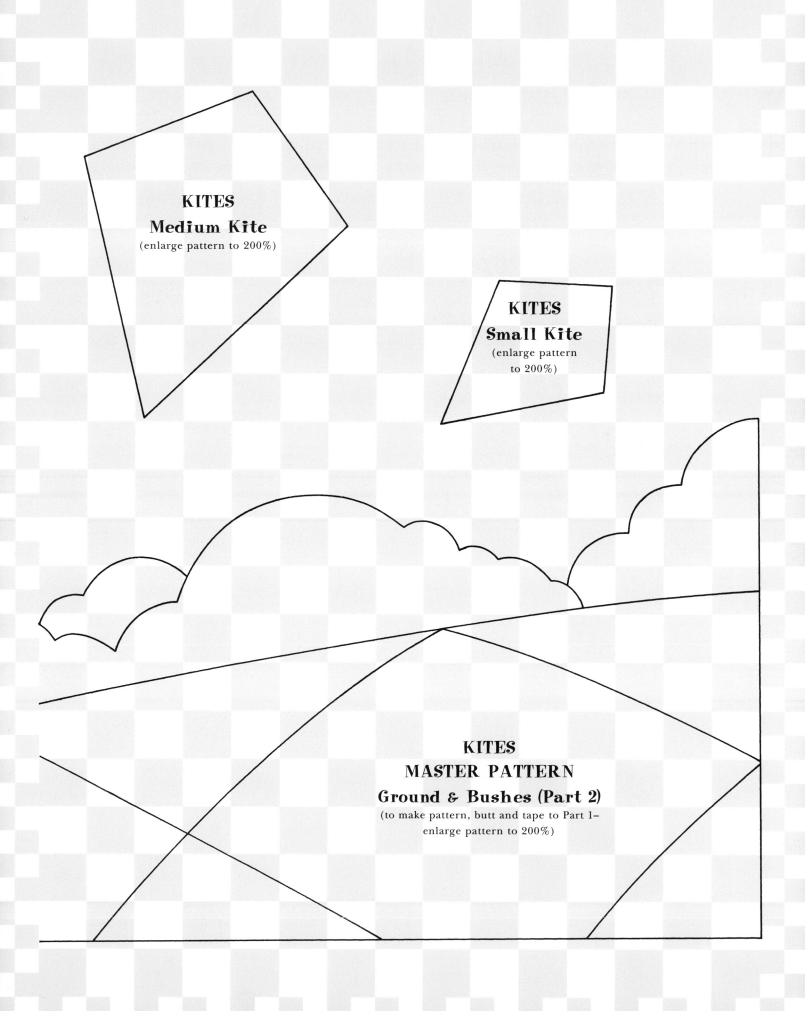

KITES
Medium Kite
(enlarge pattern to 200%)

KITES
Small Kite
(enlarge pattern
to 200%)

KITES
MASTER PATTERN
Ground & Bushes (Part 2)
(to make pattern, butt and tape to Part 1–
enlarge pattern to 200%)

PINWHEELS

✤ ✤ Size: 36" × 48" (91 × 122cm)

Wind or a child's breath will send a pinwheel into a spiraling swirl of color.
Here, the quilted variety have been frozen in midspin, and the cheerful colors of
the pinwheels and the strip-pieced border will brighten any day.

materials

- ▦ **1 yd (1m) of primarily white print (I used a light gray and white "ice" print.)**
- ▦ **¼ yd (23cm) each of six different prints and six matching solids (I used 1930s-type prints in pink, orange, blue, purple, green, and yellow.)**
- ▦ **Additional ½ yd (46cm) of orange solid fabric for borders and binding**
- ▦ **½ yd (46cm) of brown fabric**
- ▦ **1¾ yds (1.5m) of white fabric for pieced borders and backing**
- ▦ **Batting (Poly-Fil Traditional)**
- ▦ **Nylon monofilament and white threads**
- ▦ **Prizm Hologram thread, silver**
- ▦ **Bias tape maker, ½" (1.5cm)**
- ▦ **Water-soluble basting glue or glue stick for use on fabrics**
- ▦ **Template material**
- ▦ **Ruler**

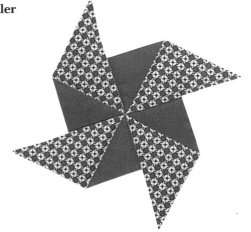

Cut six 1" (2.5cm) bias strips from brown fabric in these approximate lengths: 12" (30.5cm), 17" (43cm), 18" (45cm), 23" (58cm), 29" (74cm), and 34" (86cm). Feed through bias tape maker and iron to set folds.

From orange, cut four strips 1" (2.5cm) wide by the width of the fabric (44/45" [112/114cm]) for inner borders, and five strips 3¼" (8cm) wide for binding. Square up ¼ yd (23cm) cuts of prints and solids and cut a 1½" (4cm) strip the width of each fabric (44/45" [112/114cm]). Sew these strips together to create a composite piece of fabric from which border triangles will be cut at a later time.

Trace triangle patterns on page 73 to template material and cut out. For pinwheels, cut four large triangles from each print and four small triangles from each solid. Referring to photo as necessary, sew one solid triangle to one coordinating print triangle. Sew assembled pieces together to form a pinwheel. Press seams in one direction. Finger-press, then iron remaining outer seam allowances to wrong side of pinwheel.

Trim white print fabric to 32" × 44" (81 × 112cm). Following placement diagram on page 72, transfer markings for sticks to approximate positions on background fabric (background fabric is larger than actually needed, leaving margins for error all around). Glue brown bias tape sticks in place over guide lines on background fabric with basting glue. (Use the ruler as a guide to keep the stitches straight.) Let glue dry according to manufacturer's directions. With machine set for narrow zigzag, and top

threaded with monofilament, stitch over edges of sticks, adjusting tension if necessary so bobbin thread does not show on top. Following placement diagram on page 72, arrange pinwheels over top of sticks and glue in place with basting glue. When dry, stitch in place, as for sticks.

Centering the pinwheels, trim assembled center panel to 29½" × 41½" (75 × 105cm). Sewing on the bias, join two orange border (1" [2.5cm] wide) strips in pairs. Divide each into two pieces approximately 36" × 50" (91 × 124cm) long. Sew longer pieces to sides, shorter pieces to top and bottom of center panel, mitering the corner.

Using border triangle pattern, cut twenty-four full triangles from composite fabric. You may need to piece some from the corner pieces cut off in the process. Also from the corner pieces, cut eight slightly larger than half triangles for end pieces of border. From white fabric, cut twenty-eight full triangles. Stitch together alternately, white and pieced triangles to complete two strips with five pieced triangles and two strips with seven pieced triangles, each ending with a pieced half triangle on either end. Sew pieced border strips to edges of top, matching short to short and long to long and mitering the corners.

Press assembled quilt top and mark for quilting. Around pinwheels, mark lines ¼" (6mm) from edge, ½" (1.5cm) beyond the first line, then 1" (4cm) beyond that. Where these lines meet lines from other pinwheels, join the lines so quilting lines may encircle two or more pinwheels. Do not cross quilting lines. When pinwheels have been marked, mark straight lines parallel to sticks and approximately 1" (2.5cm) apart on all remaining unmarked areas.

Lay out backing fabric right side down. Smooth batting over backing. Center quilt top, right side up, onto batting and backing and smooth out as flat as possible. Baste or pin the layers together. With machine threaded with white, and using walking foot, stitch first in the ditch (see page 15) around and through all pinwheels and sticks. Then quilt on marked lines around pinwheels and parallel to sticks. Stitch in the ditch on either side of orange borders and along seam between white and pieced border triangles.

Smooth quilt flat and trim excess batting and backing to ¼" (6mm) beyond edges of top. Sewing on the bias, join three of the 3¼" (8cm) binding strips and divide in half. Folding binding strips in half lengthwise, wrong si together, having raw edges even and using a ½" (1.5cm) seam, sew binding strips to right side of quilt. Miter the corners. Fold binding to wrong side and slipstitch in place to seam line.

Lay out quilt and with needle and a brightly colored thread, baste guidelines as desired for wind quilting lines on center panel only. With hologram thread threaded through the top and machine set on a slightly longer stitch length, stitch close to basted lines. I basted long looping lines coming from right side of quilt. When stitching with hologram thread, I made two lines around each basted line. Don't be concerned about following the line exactly, an overall loose and loopy effect is what is desired. Remove basting thread.

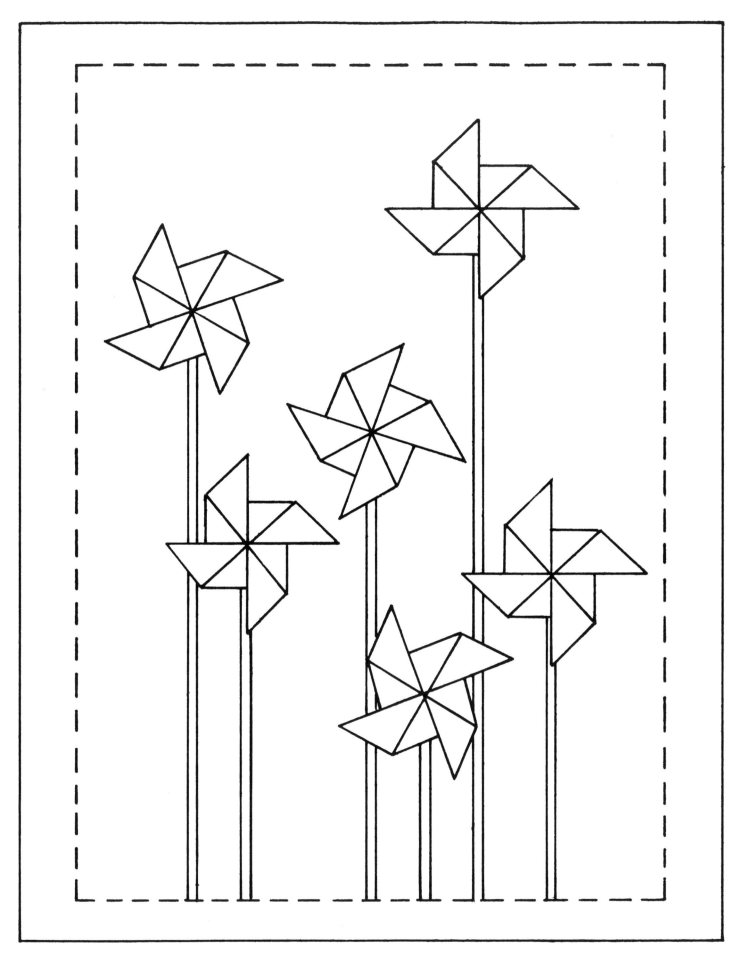

Placement Diagram

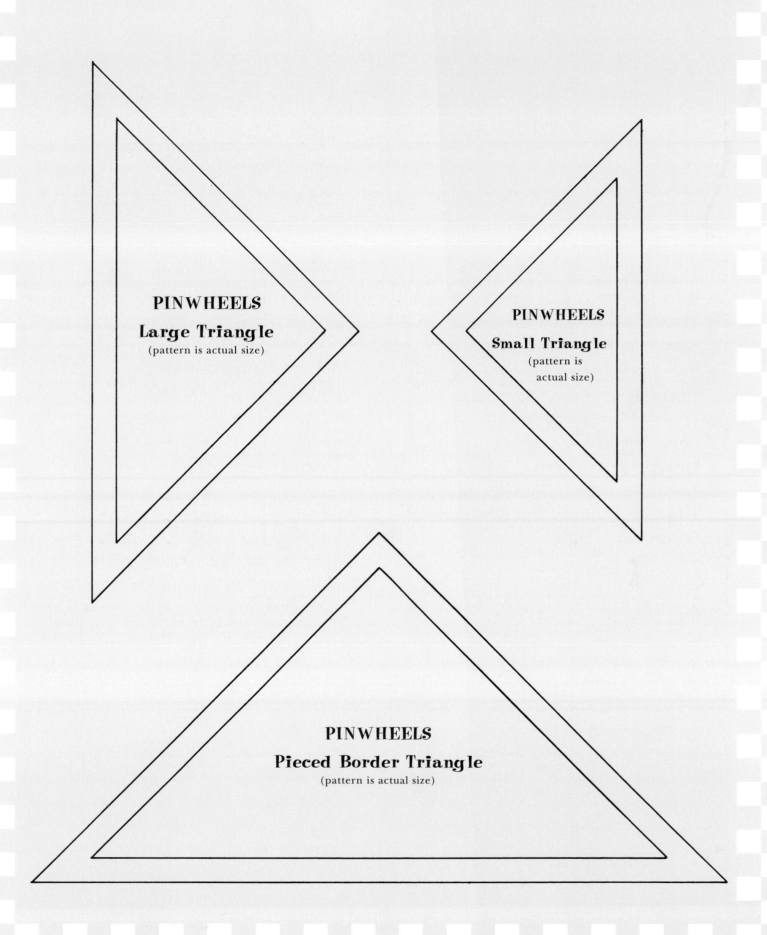

PINWHEELS

Large Triangle

(pattern is actual size)

PINWHEELS

Small Triangle

(pattern is
actual size)

PINWHEELS

Pieced Border Triangle

(pattern is actual size)

S N O W Y   D A Y

✤ ✤ SIZE: 36" × 48" (91 × 122CM)

There is a different sort of magic to be found on a winter's day when sparkling snowflakes flutter down from the skies. This quilt mimics that sparkling effect.

m a t e r i a l s

- ❖ **3 yds (3m) of blue fabric (for backing)**
- ❖ **1½ yd (1.5m) of white on white print**
- ❖ **1½ yd (1.5m) of lightweight paper-backed, fusible adhesive**
- ❖ **1 yd (1m) of tear-away stabilizer**
- ❖ **Batting (Poly-Fil Cotton Classic)**
- ❖ **Paper for enlarging patterns**
- ❖ **Matching threads (I used Sulky's Metallic Embroidery Thread, Prism White, and Silver Metallic Thread, Opalescent.)**
- ❖ **Safety pins**

From white on white print, cut four strips 3¼" (8cm) by the length of the fabric (1½ yds [1.5m]) and set aside.

Snowflake patterns given represent one-eighth of entire pattern. For each snowflake measure longest side and cut a paper square slightly more than twice as large. Fold paper into quarters, then each side back to meet the fold, dividing it into eighths. Transfer pattern to folded paper and cut out through all folds. Place paper snowflake onto paper backing of fusible adhesive and trace all edges. Following manufacturer's directions, fuse adhesive to wrong side of white on white print. Cut out snowflakes along marked lines.

Cut blue fabric in half and trim one piece to approximately 38" × 50" (97 × 127cm). Arrange snowflakes on fabric following photograph of finished quilt on next page or as desired, keeping in mind the eventual finished size of quilt. Work with one snowflake at a time, marking centers of others with a safety pin. Fuse snowflake to background fabric. Cut a square of stabilizer slightly larger than snowflake. Pin or baste stabilizer to back of fused snowflake. With machine set on medium-width zigzag and threaded with white (or other) in top, satin stitch around all edges of snowflake. Take care to enclose cut edges as they will eventually pull up if you haven't done a thorough job. Repeat for remaining snowflakes. Carefully tear away excess stabilizer. Trim finished top to 36" × 48" (91 × 122cm).

Lay remaining blue fabric out flat, right side down. Smooth batting over backing. Center finished top, right side up, onto batting and backing. Baste layers together. Stitch in the ditch (see page 15) around each snowflake and inside larger openings. Echo quilt around snowflakes with lines approximately 1" (2.5cm) apart, joining lines as they meet, so you are eventually encircling several snowflakes as you sew. When quilting is complete, trim batting and backing even with quilt top. Fold binding strips in half lengthwise, wrong sides together. With raw edges even, sew binding to right side of quilt using a ½" (1.5cm) seam. Miter corners. Turn folded edge to back of quilt and slipstitch in place over seam line.

SNOWFLAKE PATTERNS

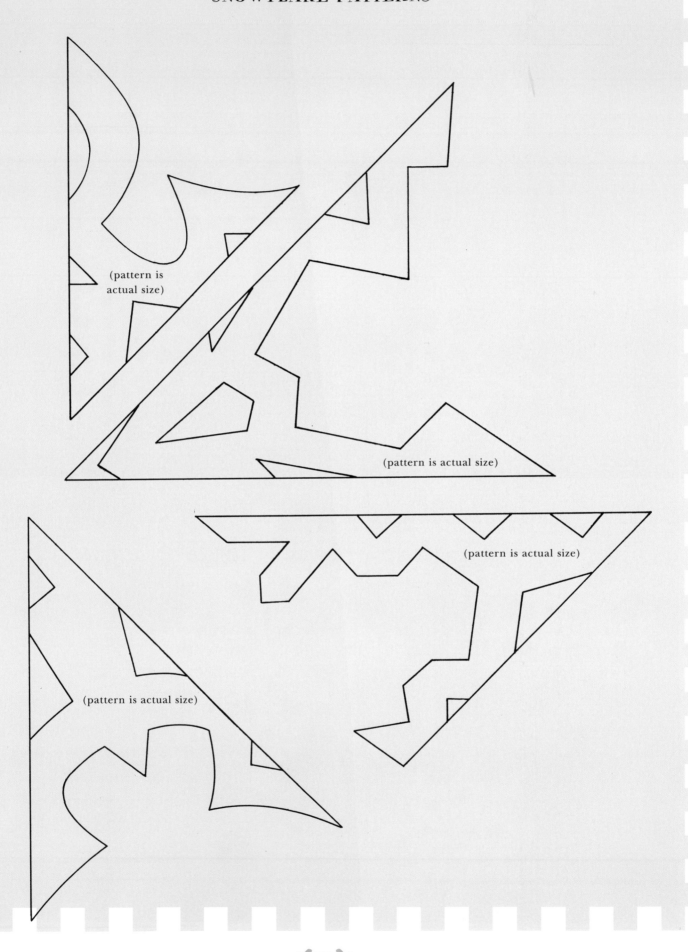

(pattern is actual size)

(pattern is actual size)

(pattern is actual size)

(pattern is actual size)

SNOWFLAKE PATTERNS

(pattern is actual size)

(pattern is actual size)

(pattern is actual size)

PERFECT

CHAPTER FIVE

PIECING

SQUARES ON SQUARES

✤ SIZE: 37" × 49" (94 × 124 CM)

Bold black and white patterns are the first things babies can see, making this quilt ideal to welcome a new arrival. The splashes of bright color at each intersection liven up the black and white prints and make this quilt a bold addition to the nursery.

materials

- **Eight ¼ yd (23cm) pieces of assorted black and white prints in a range of tones from light to dark**
- **Assorted scraps of brightly colored fabrics**
- **1½ yds (1.5m) of black fabric (backing and binding)**
- **Batting (Mountain Mist Quilt Light)**
- **Black thread**
- **¼ yd (23cm) of paper-backed fusible adhesive**
- **¾ yd (69cm) of tearaway stabilizer**

Cut each of the black and white fabrics into six 6½" (16.5cm) squares for a total of forty-eight squares. Lay

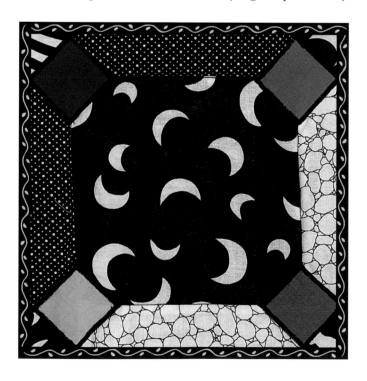

out the squares on a flat surface and arrange them as desired into eight rows of six squares each. Join the squares into rows using a ¼" (6mm) seams, then join the rows taking care to line up seam lines. Press quilt top flat.

On paper backing of the fusible adhesive, mark thirty-five 1½" (4cm) squares. Cut out squares. Following manufacturer's directions, fuse to brightly colored fabrics. Trim fabric to edge of fusible adhesive. Arrange colored squares, lined up on the diagonal, on top of seams between black and white squares. Fuse colored squares in place. Cut stabilizer into thirty-five 4" (10cm) squares and pin one behind each fused square. With machine set on medium-width zigzag and threaded with black, satin stitch around each colored square, taking care to have the bulk of the stitching on the colored square.

Lay the backing fabric wrong side down on a flat surface. Smooth the batting over the backing. Center the quilt top, right side up, on top of the batting and backing. Baste the layers together. Quilt along the seam lines between black and white squares and around each colored square. Using presser foot as a guide, stitch ¼" (6mm) from outside edge of quilt top. Trim batting to ½" (1.5cm) beyond quilt top. Trim backing fabric to 1" (2.5cm) beyond batting. Bring edges of backing to front, turning under ¼" (6mm) on raw edges and pin in place over raw edges of quilt top. Slipstitch folded edge in place to front of quilt, just over stitching line.

OLD MAID

✤ SIZE: 37" × 49" (94 × 124CM)

A curiously named pattern from quilting's long and storied past, here six blocks are set on point inside a sunny yellow border. The retro prints of the center are echoed in the outer border to create a charming quilt that works equally well for a boy or a girl.

materials

- 3 yds (3m) of unbleached muslin for top and back
- ¼ yd (23cm) cuts of assorted 1930s-type prints (I used at least twelve different prints, but it is not necessary to use that many)
- 1 yd (1m) of yellow fabric
- Batting (Fairfield Soft Touch Cotton)
- Thread, ivory
- Tracing paper
- Template material

From muslin, cut two strips 6½" × 34" (17 × 86cm), two strips 6½" × 44" (17 × 112cm), and two 7½" (19cm) squares and set aside.

On paper, draft two 7" (18cm) squares. Divide one square in half diagonally from corner to corner, then one triangle in half again from corner of square to center point of first diagonal line. Trace larger and smaller triangles to template material adding ¼" (6mm) seam allowance all around, and cut out. With these two triangle patterns, cut four small triangles and six large triangles from muslin and set aside.

Referring to piecing diagram, divide second square into quarters. Divide one quarter in half diagonally for

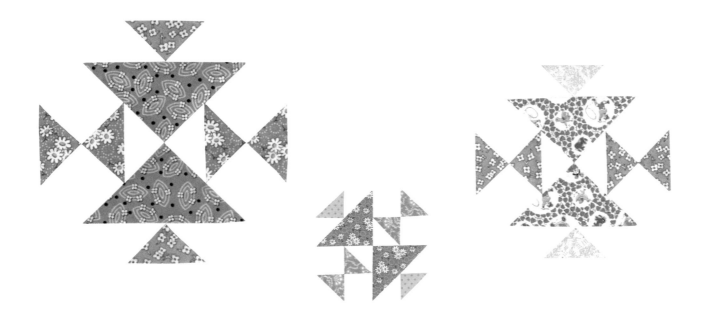

large triangle and one quarter into quarters again for small square, and lastly, one small square in half diagonally for small triangle. Trace one each, large and small triangles and small square, to template material, again adding ¼" (6mm) seam allowance all around. Using small square pattern on page 86, cut twenty-four from muslin. Using large triangle pattern on page 86, cut six pairs from assorted print fabrics. Using small triangle pattern on page 86, cut six sets of four matching triangles (A pieces), six pairs of triangles (B pieces) from assorted prints, and sixty triangles from muslin. Using ¼" (6mm) seam allowance, sew all print triangles to muslin triangles along longest side. Separate into A piece squares and B piece squares. Sew additional muslin triangle to each side of B piece squares, referring to piecing diagram on page 86 as necessary, to form large triangles. Sew these assembled large triangles in matching pairs to matching pairs of large print triangles along longest side.

Sew small muslin squares to assembled A squares, taking care to align the muslin square to the same side of each pieced square. Join these units in patched pairs into squares with print triangles meeting in a bow tie at the center (refer to piecing diagram on page 86 as necessary).

The large pieced squares will now be joined to form each Old Maid block according to piecing diagram; take care to match up pairs of prints in each unit. Referring to assembly diagram on page 87, join pieced blocks with muslin squares and triangles cut earlier, to form rows, then join rows to form the center panel.

From yellow fabric, cut four inner border strips, two 1¼" × 22" (3 × 56cm) and two 1¼" × 33" (3 × 84cm). With right sides together and raw edges even, sew shorter strips centered on short ends of center panel, beginning and ending ¼" (6mm) from edges. Sew remaining strips to sides in the same manner. Miter the corners and trim excess fabric. Center shorter muslin strips on shorter ends and longer strips on longer sides of center panel and sew in same manner as yellow border strips, again mitering the corners along same line as previous corners.

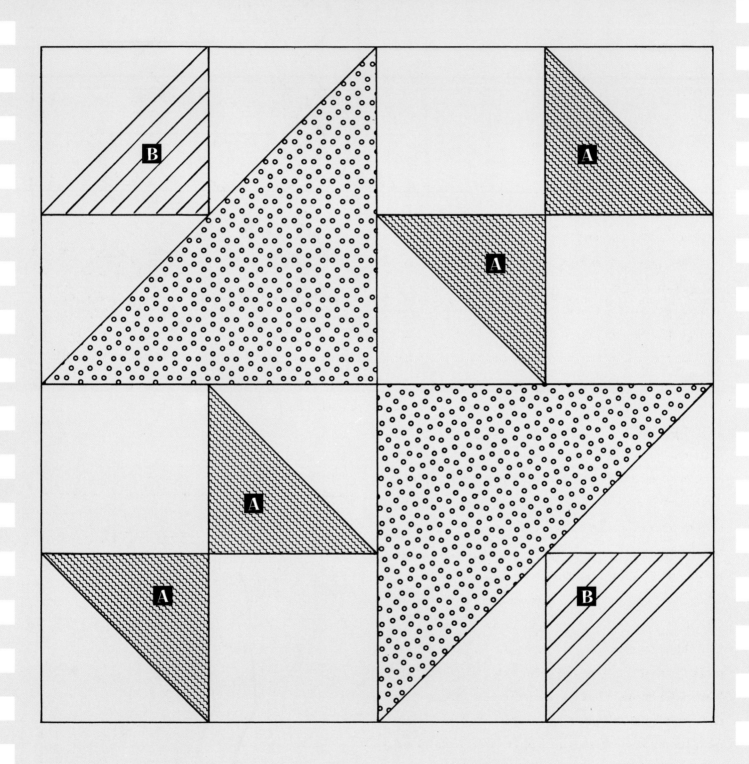

Trace border triangle pattern to template material, adding ¼" (6mm) seam allowances all around. Cut fifty from assorted prints and forty-six from muslin. Sew two strips alternating eleven print and ten muslin triangles each and two strips with fourteen print and thirteen muslin triangles each. With right sides together, pin shorter strips to shorter sides of quilt top, longer strips to longer sides and sew in place—each strip should fit exactly to length of muslin border with ¼" (6mm) allowance to miter the corner. Line up mitered corners with the previous miters.

On quilt top, with a long ruler and pencil, lightly mark quilting lines diagonally across muslin borders from tip of one triangle on one side of corner to its partner on the other side of the corner. Move the ruler up to the next set of triangle points and connect them. Continue in this manner to mark parallel lines from triangle tip to triangle tip until entire muslin border is marked diagonally into squares. Lay backing (remaining muslin) out right side down on flat surface. Smooth batting over backing. Center quilt top, right side up, onto batting and backing. Baste layers together. With machine threaded with ivory thread, quilt around larger triangles in pieced squares and around outside of largest squares. Quilt around inside and outside of yellow border, outside of muslin border and up and down each border triangle seam, along marked quilting lines on border, and lastly, down mitered seam of muslin border through pieced triangle border. Trim batting and backing to ½" (1.5cm) beyond quilt top.

From remaining yellow fabric cut five binding strips each 4¾" (12cm) wide by the width of the fabric (44/45" [112/114cm]). Sew three of those strips together on the bias and cut this strip in half. With wrong sides together, fold binding strips in half lengthwise and pin shorter strips to shorter edges, longer strips to longer edges of quilt front having raw edges even. Sew, using ¾" (2cm) seam and stopping ¾" (2cm) from each edge of quilt. Miter the corners, and trim excess fabric. Turn folded edge to back and slipstitch in place just over seam line.

Assembly Diagram

OLD MAID

Border Triangle
(pattern is actual size)
Seam allowances included

HARLEQUIN JACKET, HAT, AND BOOTIES

SIZE: TO FIT APPROXIMATELY 6–12 MONTHS. ✚ ✚ JACKET MEASURES APPROXIMATELY 22" (56CM) AROUND CHEST. ✚ ✚ HAT MEASURES APPROXIMATELY 18" (45.5CM) AROUND LOWER BRIM. ✚ ✚ BOOTIES MEASURE APPROXIMATELY 4¾" (12CM) FROM HEEL TO TOE.

A variety of bright and boldly patterned fabrics brings a harlequin feel to these tiny garments. A jacket with overlapping fronts to make it extra cozy, booties with ribbed cuffs to help them stay on, and a charming little hat combine to make a darling outfit for a lucky infant.

materials

- **1 yd (1m) each of black and gray prints**
- **½ yd (46cm) of black and white stripe fabric**
- **Assorted ¼ yd (23cm) cuts of bright prints (I used five different prints)**
- **6" × 7" (15 × 18cm) piece of matching ribbing**
- **Scraps of low loft batting (Poly-Fil Low Loft Batting)**
- **Matching threads and rayon machine embroidery thread, light gray**
- **Nylon monofilament thread for machine quilting**
- **Small piece template material**
- **Clear plastic quilting ruler with 60-degree markings**
- **Five black Velcro fasteners for closing jacket**

JACKET

Enlarge jacket pattern pieces on page 93. Trace diamond pattern to template material. (The ¼" [6mm] seam allowances are already included for these.) Cut out template and use to cut approximately forty diamonds from assorted bright fabrics. Join diamonds into larger piece of fabric by assembling two strips of seven and one strip each of six, five, three, and two diamonds. As you assemble this pieced fabric, keep referring back to jacket front pattern piece to determine if you have all edges covered with a little margin for error. When you are done piecing, press the assembled fabric and cut matching pieces from black fabric and batting. Sandwich the batting between the layers of fabric, securing with a few straight pins. With machine threaded with nylon on top, black in bobbin, quilt along seam lines of pieced fabric.

Cut one piece each of gray print fabric, batting, and black fabric approximately 1" (2.5cm) larger all around than each jacket pattern piece, cutting two sleeve pieces of each fabric. With a marking tool that will show up on the gray fabric, mark it into 1½" (4cm) diamonds (start with parallel lines 1½" [4cm] apart and divide them into diamonds), using the 60-degree marking on your quilting ruler to get the proper angles. These diamonds should be the same size as the pieced diamonds. Layer each marked piece over matching batting and black fabric pieces, securing the layers with straight pins. With machine threaded on top with light gray rayon machine embroidery thread and black in bobbin, quilt along marked lines. Cut jacket pieces from quilted pieces, taking care to reverse front pattern to cut a left and right piece. Clean-finish side, armhole, and shoulder edges of jacket fronts, and back, side, and top edges of sleeves with zigzag stitching. Join jacket fronts to back at shoulders using a ½" (1.5cm) seam. Sew sleeves into armholes, also

using ½" (1.5cm) seam. With same size seam, sew side and sleeve seams from bottom of jacket to underarm, then from bottom of sleeve to underarm.

From striped fabric, cut several strips 1¾" (4cm) wide by the width of the fabric (44/45" [112/114cm]). With wrong sides together, fold one strip in half lengthwise and turn back ½" (1.5cm) at beginning of strip. Pin folded end to right side of sleeve hem at underarm seam having raw edges even. Using a ¼" (6mm) seam, sew strip around sleeve, overlapping folded end at point where you began. Turn folded edge to inside and slipstitch in place just over seam line. Repeat for other sleeve hem. Join two additional strips of striped fabric and fold in half lengthwise wrong sides together. Beginning at upper left corner of jacket front, having raw edges even and using ¼" (6mm) seams, pin and sew strip around neck edge, down right front edge, around back, and back up left front, turning under end to create a neat finish on this final corner. As you turn each corner, stop ¼" (6mm) from edge, fold strip up off work at right angle to seam just sewn, then fold strip back down even with next edge and continue sewing, starting ¼" (6mm) from that edge. This creates a very neat mitered corner with surprisingly little effort. Turn folded edge to inside and slipstitch in place over seam line. Stitch loop portion of Velcro fastener to top and bottom corners of inside right front edge. Stitch two more loop portions equally spaced between the first two. Sew hook portions of Velcro to left front, opposite loop portions. Sew remaining hook portion to upper corner of left front, sewing matching loop portion to inside right front opposite hook portion.

B O O T I E S

Trace bootie uppers and sole patterns on page 94 to paper. Seam allowances are already included. From assorted prints, cut thirty-six 2" (5cm) squares. Using ¼" (6mm) seam, assemble squares into nine rows of four squares each. Sew the rows together, taking care to line up the seams. Press the assembled fabric. Cut a matching piece of

batting and black fabric and pin the layers together. With machine threaded with nylon on top, black in bobbin, quilt along all seam lines.

Cut one 8" × 9" (20 × 23cm) piece of gray print, black fabric, and batting. Mark the gray print fabric into 1½" (4cm) squares set on the diagonal. With machine threaded on top with light gray rayon machine embroidery thread and black in the bobbin, quilt along marked lines.

Cut two sole pieces from gray quilted fabric marking center back, two upper pieces from pieced fabric. From striped fabric, cut a strip 1" (2.5cm) wide by the width of the fabric. Cut ribbing into two pieces each 3½" × 6" (9 × 15cm) with the ribbing running along the shorter measurement. Pin long edge of ribbing, right sides together, to inside curve of bootie upper, stretching it to fit. Sew using a ¼" (6mm) seam. With right sides together, sew center back seam of bootie upper and ribbing. Turning under ¼" (6mm) on raw edge, fold ribbing to inside and slipstitch over seam line, enclosing raw edges.

With right sides together and folding under end at beginning, pin striped strip around bottom edge of bootie

upper, starting and ending at center back. Using a ¼"
(6mm) seam, sew strip to upper, then sew opposite side of
strip to bootie sole, right sides together and lining up center
back marking with center back seam of bootie upper.
Turn under ¼" (6mm) on either side of remaining striped
strip and sew by hand inside bootie, enclosing raw edges
where striped strip was joined to outside of bootie.

HAT

Trace small brim pattern piece to template material and
cut out. Cut six crown pieces each from gray print, black
fabric, and batting. Using ¼" (6mm) seams, join gray
pieces along long edges, and then black pieces in the
same manner. Trim seam allowances from long edges of
batting pieces and join them, butted together, by hand
using a large overcast stitch. With the black crown assembly inside out, place the batting crown over it, and the
gray crown over that, right side out. Pin the layers together, matching the seams on the black and gray print layers
as much as possible. With machine threaded with light
gray rayon machine embroidery thread on top, black in
the bobbin, sew along seam lines of gray layer of crown,
working from outside edge into the center.

Transfer hat brim lining, outer brim, and crown patterns from page 95 to paper. Seam allowances have
already been included. Using small brim template on
page 95, cut twelve from assorted prints. Join them, using
¼" (6mm) seams along side (straight) edges to form
brim. Using brim lining pattern, cut one each, on fold as
indicated, from black fabric and batting. Trim seam
allowance from short ends of batting and join as for
crown. Using ¼" (6mm) seam, sew short ends of black
brim lining. Place batting between pieced brim and black
brim lining; pin together. From striped fabric, cut a strip
1¾" (4.5cm) wide by the width of the fabric (44/45"
[112/114cm]). With wrong sides together, fold strip in
half lengthwise and turn under ½" (1.5cm) at the beginning. Pin strip to right side of brim at upper edge. Using
a ¼" (6mm) seam, sew to brim edge. Turn folded edge to
back and slipstitch in place over seam line.

Having right side of brim facing wrong side of crown,
pin only the right side of brim and batting to the crown of
the hat. Sew using a ¼" (6mm) seam. Fold under raw edge
of brim lining and slipstitch in place over seam line,
enclosing raw edges. With machine threaded with nylon
on top, black in bobbin, quilt along seam lines between
pieces on brim.

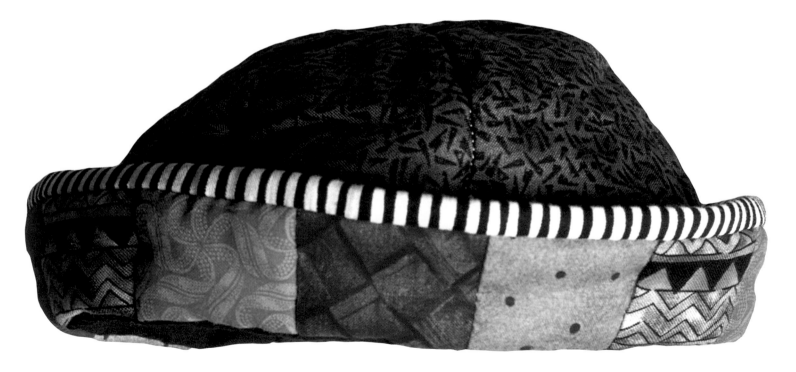

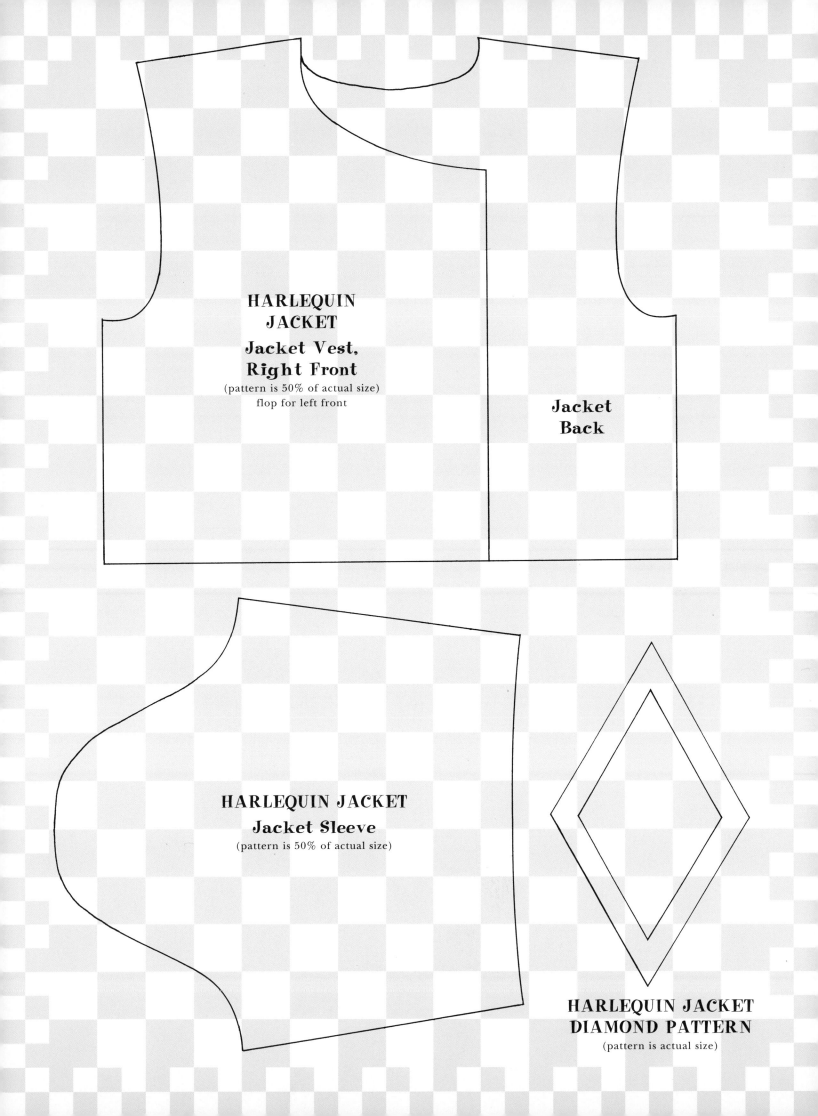

HARLEQUIN JACKET

Jacket Vest, Right Front

(pattern is 50% of actual size)
flop for left front

Jacket Back

HARLEQUIN JACKET

Jacket Sleeve

(pattern is 50% of actual size)

HARLEQUIN JACKET DIAMOND PATTERN

(pattern is actual size)

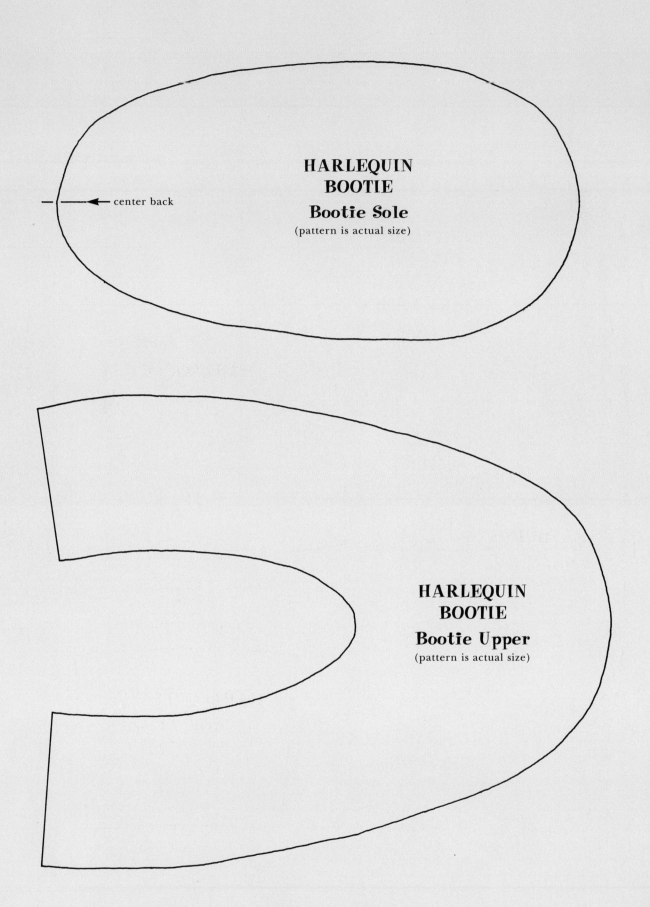

HARLEQUIN BOOTIE

Bootie Sole

(pattern is actual size)

← center back

HARLEQUIN BOOTIE

Bootie Upper

(pattern is actual size)

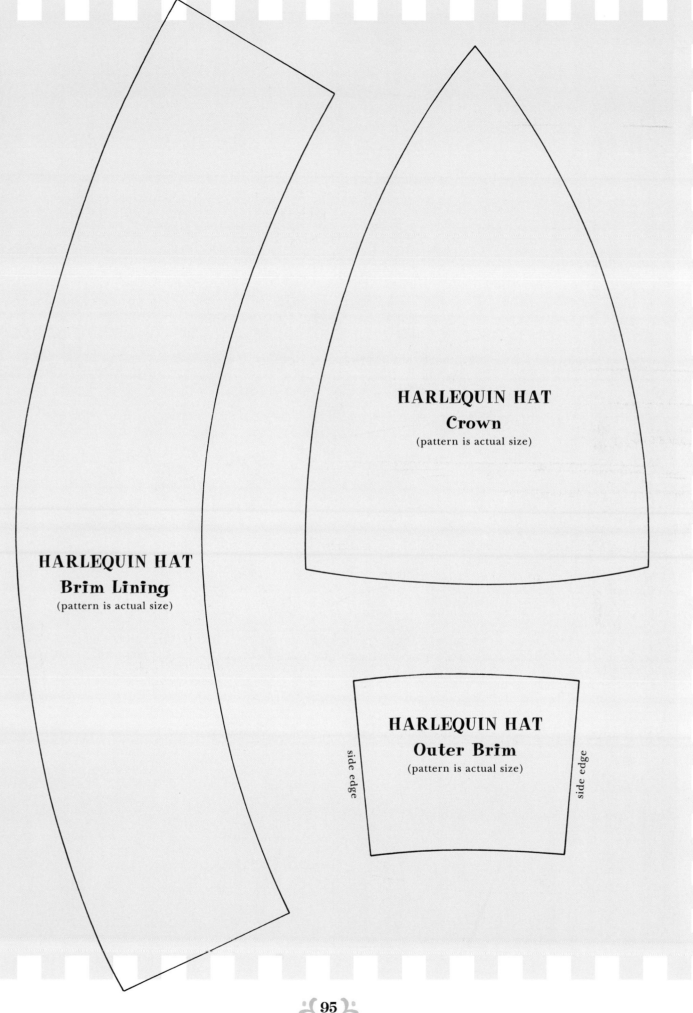

HARLEQUIN HAT

Crown

(pattern is actual size)

HARLEQUIN HAT

Brim Lining

(pattern is actual size)

HARLEQUIN HAT

Outer Brim

(pattern is actual size)

side edge

side edge

SOUTHWESTERN STAR

Bold tones of purple, red, orange, and turquoise become electrified when set against black in this striking arrangement that evokes Southwestern Native American blankets.

materials

- ❖ **1 yd (1m) of black fabric**
- ❖ **½ yd (46cm) each of red, turquoise, purple, and orange prints**
- ❖ **1½ yd (1.5m) of backing fabric**
- ❖ **Batting (Poly-Fil Cotton Classic)**
- ❖ **Matching thread and nylon monofilament thread for quilting**

For center medallion, cut five black and twelve turquoise 2½" (6.5cm) squares. Using medium triangle pattern on page 99, cut eight each black and turquoise print triangles. Sew black triangles to turquoise triangles to form eight pieced 2½" (6.5cm) squares. Press.

Sew squares together using the following instructions. Strip 1 (make two): turquoise, pieced, turquoise, pieced, turquoise. Strip 2 (make two): pieced, black, turquoise, black, pieced. Strip 3 (make one): turquoise, turquoise, black, turquoise, turquoise. Sew strips together: 1 to 2 to 3 to 2 to 1. Refer to photograph of finished quilt on page 96 for proper placement of squares and strips. From turquoise, cut four 1½" × 12½" (4 × 32cm) strips. Sew one strip to each side of assembled piece, mitering corners. Press and trim medallion to 12" (30cm) square.

From black, cut five binding strips each 3¼" (8cm) wide by the width of fabric (44/45" [112/114cm]) and set aside. Using medium triangle pattern on page 99, cut 204 from black fabric. From orange print fabric, cut twenty-four 2½" (6.5cm) squares. Sew one black triangle to top and bottom of each square, reversing right angle corner of triangle top and bottom to create a long diamond shape. Sew these pieces together, having top of one square line up with bottom of next square to make a strip of orange print diamonds surrounded by black triangles. Make four strips of six diamonds each. Press accurately. Mark center of each strip (the point where third and fourth diamonds meet) and center of each medallion side. Having center points matched, sew strips to each side of medallion, mitering corners and taking care to have all seams along the mitered edge aligned. Press assembled square. Mark ¼" (6mm) seam line around piece and press seam allowances to the wrong side.

From red print, cut a 14½" × 27½" (37 × 70cm) strip. From purple print, cut two strips, each 7" × 27½" (18 × 70cm). From orange print, cut two strips, each 4½" × 27½" (11 × 70cm). From remaining red and orange prints, and using small triangle pattern, cut forty-eight pieces each. Cut ninety-six small triangles from purple print.

Sew one purple triangle to each of the orange and red triangles along longest side. For each color combination, join assembled squares into four strips of twelve each, two with one color triangle facing right and two with the same color triangle facing left. Referring to photograph on page 96 if necessary, join pairs of mirror image strips,

one medium black triangle to each short side of large turquoise triangles. Press carefully so as not to distort resulting rectangle. Assemble rectangles into four strips of six and four strips of nine each having points of all turquoise triangles facing in the same direction.

From purple print fabric and using large triangle pattern on page 99, cut sixteen pieces. Assemble with black triangles as above and press. Stitch two assembled rectangles together so that purple triangles form a square in the center. Sew one short turquoise pieced strip to either end of two purple diamonds. Sew one purple diamond to each end of these strips. Sew one long turquoise pieced strip to either end of two remaining purple diamonds. Sew longer strips to each side of pieced center panel and shorter strips across each end. Press.

Mark quilt top for quilting. The center panel, outside of the medallion, should be quilted in diagonal lines that take their direction from the sawtooth borders and so echo the outline of the medallion. The quilting lines reverse direction, making a right angle along the center line of the purple band to head off in the same direction as the triangles in the purple/orange sawtooth border. You should end up with lines ¾"–⅞" (2cm) apart and running at a 45-degree angle to the straight lines in the quilt top.

Lay backing fabric out right side down. Smooth batting on top of backing. Center top, right side up, onto batting and backing. Baste layers together. With monofilament threaded in top of machine, stitch in the ditch

so red and orange triangles meet in the center forming larger triangles.

Stitch one pieced red and purple strip to each long side of 14½" × 27½" (11 × 70cm) red print strip having edges of small red triangles bordering red print strip to create sawtooth border.

Sew one purple strip to each side of pieced red/purple strip. Sew purple/orange pieced strips to edges of purple strips. Sew orange strips to opposite sides of purple and orange sawtooth borders. Press assembled piece.

Lay center panel out flat and mark the center by folding in half along length and width of panel. Align corners of center medallion along fold lines and pin in place along all edges. By hand, appliqué center medallion in place.

Using large triangle pattern on page 99, cut sixty from remaining turquoise print fabric. Join long side of around black star in center of medallion, inside and outside of medallion's diamond border, and around each orange diamond in that border. (See page 15). Quilt on marked lines on remainder of center panel, then along edge of outer border and around each triangle and diamond in that border. Trim batting and backing to ¼" (6mm) beyond top. Sew three of the black binding strips together on the bias, then cut in half. With wrong sides together, fold binding strips in half lengthwise. With raw edges even, stitch to right side of quilt using a ½" (1.5cm) seam. Miter corners. Turn folded edge of binding to back and slipstitch just over seam line.

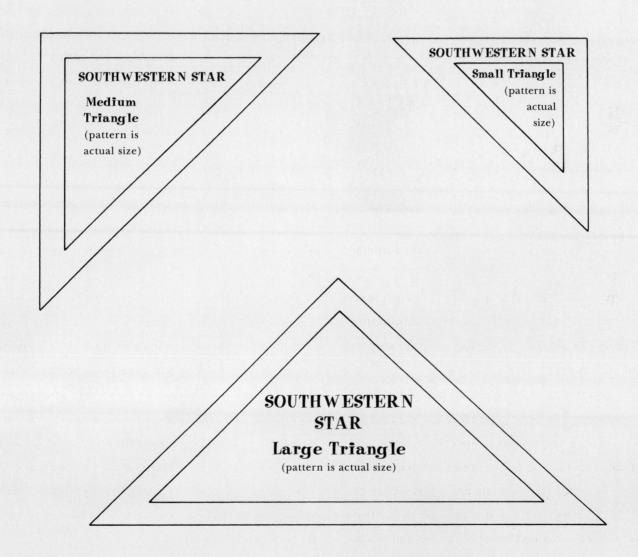

SOUTHWESTERN STAR

Medium
Triangle
(pattern is
actual size)

SOUTHWESTERN STAR

Small Triangle
(pattern is
actual
size)

SOUTHWESTERN
STAR

Large Triangle
(pattern is actual size)

¼" (6mm) seam allowances are included

HE SAID,

CHAPTER SIX

SHE SAID

A bright assortment of colorful flowers is literally bursting out of the blue checked blocks of this quilt's background, giving it a very striking appearance, while the curving outer border keeps to the frilly theme.

materials

- 1½ yds (1.5cm) of white fabric
- ¾ yd (69cm) of blue checked fabric
- 1½ yds (1.5m) of backing fabric
- Scraps of assorted bright colored fabrics, including two or more greens
- Small piece of freezer paper
- Water-soluble stabilizer
- Water-soluble basting glue
- Matching threads
- Batting (Poly-Fil Traditional)
- ½" (1.5cm) bias tape maker

Note: Take care when transferring markings to water-soluble stabilizer. When you wash the quilt for the first time to remove the stabilizer, any markings on the stabilizer may transfer themselves to the fabric. It would be wise to test out marker, fabric, and stabilizer before beginning.

From blue checked fabric, cut sixteen 6½" (16.5cm) squares. From white fabric cut two strips 2" × 52" (5 × 132cm), two strips 2" × 41" (5 × 104cm) and set aside. Cut also two strips 6½" × 24½" (16.5 × 62cm), two strips 6½" × 36½" (16.5 × 93cm), and twelve 6½" (16.5cm) squares. Sew the squares into six rows of four squares each, alternating blue check and white squares. Matching seam lines, sew the rows together, again alternating the squares, to form a checkerboard pattern. Sew one longer white piece to each long side of checkerboard assembly. Sew one remaining blue check square to each end of remaining white strips. Sew pieced strips to ends of checkerboard assembly, matching seam lines.

Trace flower and leaf patterns on page 105–106 to water-soluble stabilizer and cut apart. You will need a total of sixteen flowers and at least sixteen leaves. Match each stabilizer pattern to selected fabric and cut fabrics into general size/shape of flowers with a generous allowance on all sides (an about 6" [15cm] square will do). Trace matching flower centers to paper side of freezer paper and cut out along marked lines.

Coordinate fabrics for flower centers to their corresponding flowers. Using a dry iron set on cotton, fuse shiny/plastic side of freezer paper to wrong side of selected flower center fabrics. Cut out ⅛"–¼" (3–6mm) beyond freezer paper. Finger-press excess fabric to freezer paper side (back). Use basting glue, adhere

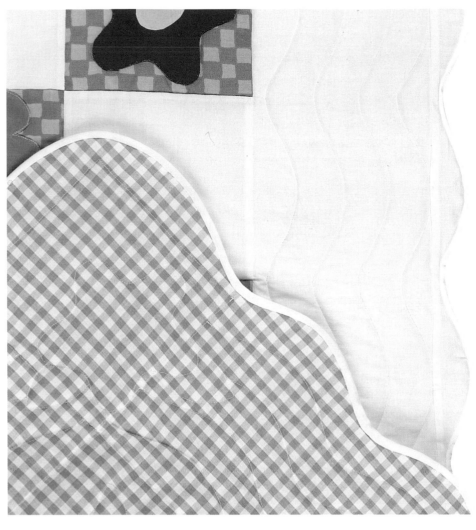

ing thread and stitching very close to edges. Re-pin flower and stitch down in the same manner.

Return to 2" (5cm)-wide white strips. Transfer border pattern to strips, having outermost curves even with edges and beginning with a corner section followed by four inner sections on shorter strips and six inner sections on longer strips and finishing with a corner section. Sew shorter and longer strips to their respective edges of assembled quilt top, mitering the corners. Use inner section of border pattern to mark quilting lines on white strips between checked corner squares. You should end up with four evenly spaced lines that echo the border.

Lay backing right side down on flat surface. Smooth batting on top of backing. Center quilt top, right side up, onto batting and backing. Baste layers together. With machine threaded with matching threads in bobbin and on top (or use nylon on top), quilt around each flower and leaf, and along seam lines around each square. Then quilt along wavy lines marked on inner borders.

From remaining white fabric, mark the bias and cut several bias strips, 1" (2.5cm) wide. Join the strips to create a piece approximately 6 yds (5.5m) long. Pull strip through the bias tape maker, using a steam iron to set folds as you go. Trim quilt borders along marked lines. Opening out one side of folded tape, pin to right side of quilt, lining up raw edges and stretching along inside curves. Fold back ½" (1.5cm) at beginning edge and stitch using a scant ¼" (6mm) seam. Turn remaining folded edge to back and slipstitch in place just over seam line, smoothing the fit around curves.

centers to the approximate center of selected flower fabrics. With machine threaded on top with matching thread, stitch as close to folded edge as possible. Turn piece over and very carefully—without cutting front fabric—cut flower fabric about ⅛" (3mm) inside stitching. Remove the freezer paper, dampening piece to release the basting glue, if necessary. Cut stabilizer flower shapes apart and pin each to right side of selected fabrics, centering the flower center within the outline. With matching thread, sew along marked lines. Trim fabric and stabilizer to ⅛"–¼" (3–6mm) beyond line, clip curves, then make a slit in stabilizer and turn flower right side out. Finger-press stabilizer to back along seam lines. Assemble leaves in the same manner. Pin flowers and leaves in place on checked squares, overlapping seam lines as desired. Lift flower from overlapping leaves and sew leaves in place first, using match-

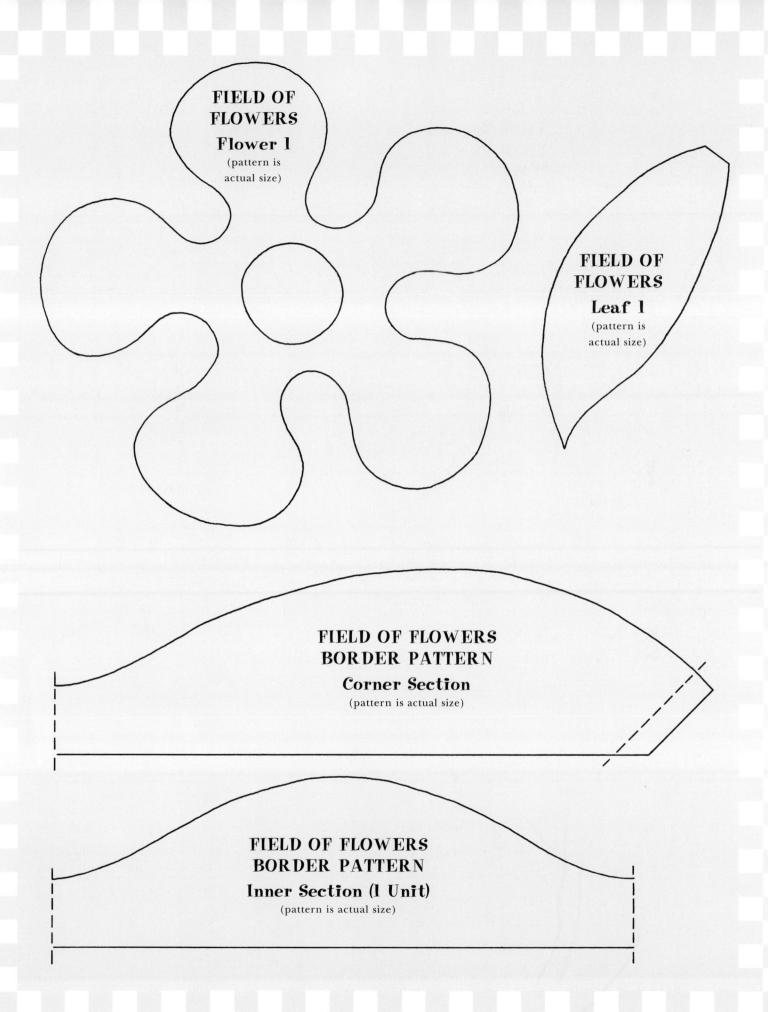

FIELD OF
FLOWERS
Flower 1
(pattern is
actual size)

FIELD OF
FLOWERS
Leaf 1
(pattern is
actual size)

FIELD OF FLOWERS
BORDER PATTERN
Corner Section
(pattern is actual size)

FIELD OF FLOWERS
BORDER PATTERN
Inner Section (1 Unit)
(pattern is actual size)

FIELD OF FLOWERS
Flower 2
(pattern is actual size)

FIELD OF FLOWERS
Leaf 2
(pattern is actual size)

FIELD OF FLOWERS
Flower 3
(pattern is actual size)

FIELD OF FLOWERS
Leaf 3
(pattern is actual size)

HEART OF MINE

✚ Size: 36" × 44½" (91 × 113cm)

Hearts have always symbolized love, and these hearts decorated
in a variety of styles may inspire you to create a quilt like this one,
full of love for a new arrival dear to your heart.

materials

- ▨ **Assorted white on white or natural prints for block backgrounds to total approximately 1 yd (1m)**
- ▨ **Assorted pink prints and solids, as desired**
- ▨ **1⅓ yds (1.5m) of dark pink print for borders**
- ▨ **1⅓ yds (1.5m) of white on white print for binding**
- ▨ **1⅓ yds (1.5m) of backing fabric**
- ▨ **Assorted notions for trimming hearts, as desired**
- ▨ **Batting (Mountain Mist Quilt-Light)**
- ▨ **White and nylon monofilament thread**
- ▨ **Water-soluble basting glue**
- ▨ **Fray check**

Note: This quilt would be most suitable as a wall hanging. The silk ribbon embroidery will not hold up well to machine washing and the various trims probably will not stand up to much wear and tear from a child's inquiring fingers. If you would like the quilt to be more functional, use only completely sewn down decorations, such as the rickrack trim.

From neutrals, cut fifteen squares each 8½" (21.5cm) and eight squares each 4½" (11cm). From pinks, cut three squares each 8½" (21.5cm). If working ribbon embroidery on any hearts, lightly sketch heart shape onto fabric and work embroidery. (See page 109 for instructions to create ribbon embroidery hearts.) When embroidery is complete, realign heart pattern and cut out, adding ¼" (6mm) seam allowance all around. Using heart patterns provided on page 111, trace large heart fifteen times to right sides of assorted pink fabrics, and three times to neutral fabrics. Cut out ¼" (6mm) beyond traced lines. Do the same with small heart pattern, cutting eight from assorted pinks. Clip seam allowance just to inside V at top of hearts and finger-press all seam allowances along traced lines to wrong side of heart. Pin hearts to centers of backing squares and hand-appliqué in place, easing in fullness around curves. Sew small hearts onto small squares and larger hearts onto larger squares.

Rickrack heart: Using basting glue, glue rickrack ½" (1.5cm) inside edge of heart. Machine stitch along center of rickrack.

about ½" (1.5cm) from center. Machine stitch along each edge of ribbon up to that point. Tie ribbon into small bow and, by hand, tack knot to heart. Trim ends of ribbon and seal edges with Fray-check.

Heart within a heart: Using pattern provided on page 111, cut one inner heart, adding seam allowances as before, from a coordinating fabric. Turn under allowances same as for larger hearts and appliqué to center of large heart.

Yo-yo flower heart: Cut three 3½" (9cm) circles from desired fabrics. Folding under ⅛"–¼" (3–6mm) as you go, baste close to folded edges. Draw up to gather tightly and fasten off thread. Cut two 1½" × 3" (4 × 8cm) rectangles of green fabric. With right sides together, fold in half with short ends together. Sew a narrow seam from fold to one short edge. Turn seam to inside and finger-press to form triangle. By hand, gather raw edges of triangle to form leaf shape. Arrange yo-yos and leaves as desired on heart. Tack in place by hand, sewing a small pearl to center of each yo-yo at the same time.

Two-color heart with embroidered trim: Sew a 4" × 6" (10 × 15cm) piece of each of two different pinks together along one long edge. Press seam to one side. Butt embroidered trim along seam and machine stitch in place along each side. Position heart pattern as desired across seam, cut out, and proceed as on previous page.

Quartered heart: Cut two 3½" (9cm) squares of each of two fabrics. Stitch one of each together along one side, then join the two pieces, reversing the placement of fabrics for checkerboard effect. Press seams to one side. Position heart pattern on pieced fabric, cut out, and appliqué as on previous page.

Ribbon bow heart: After cutting out heart, cut two 12" (30cm) lengths of ribbon and pin one under each side of heart, approximately the same distance from the top on each side. When appliquéing heart to background, take a few extra stitches to anchor ribbon in place. After appliqué is completely sewn down, use fabric glue, or pin ribbon in place to front of heart, each ribbon ending

Ribbon embroidery hearts: On desired fabric, mark outline of heart. Lightly transfer placement of embroidery inside outline as desired, using photograph on page 108 for reference. Using 4mm silk ribbon to work flowers as follows:

Violets: straight-stitch petals with purple and gold ribbon, or dark and light purples, working three straight stitches and a French knot in center of flower with purple embroidery floss. With green floss, work stem, then several ribbon-stitch leaves with green ribbon. Wider leaves are made with side by side ribbon stitches, points touching.

knot buds around roses. Larger buds are made with a medium pink lazy daisy stitch with a dark pink stitch up the middle. Join all with embroidery floss stems and straight-stitch ribbon leaves.

Using ¼" (6mm) seams, join smaller squares to form 8½" (21.5cm) squares. Decide on arrangement of appliquéd squares and stitch first in rows, then stitch rows together using ¼" (6mm) seams. From dark pink print, cut four 2½" (6.5cm)-wide border strips by length of fabric (1⅓ yds [1.2m]). Leaving excess on each end, stitch strips to each side of quilt top. Miter corners. Press.

Lay backing right side down. Smooth batting in place over backing. Lay quilt top right side up, centered on batting and backing. Baste the layers together. With machine threaded on top with monofilament, stitch in the ditch (see page 15) along all block seam lines and around each heart. Quilt also the seam line between blocks and border. Trim batting and backing to ¼" (6mm) beyond edge of quilt top.

From binding fabric, cut four 3¼" (8cm) strips, and fold in half wrong sides together. Leaving excess at ends and with raw edges even, stitch to right side of quilt using a ½" (1.5cm) seam. Miter corners to match previous mitered corners. Turn folded edge of binding to back and slipstitch in place just over the seam line.

Foxglove: Work stem with green floss, working several French knots around the top of stem, then several French knots with light purple ribbon. Then as you move down the stem, work several straight stitches for small flowers, then several ribbon stitches for somewhat larger flowers. Lastly, finish with several straight-stitch leaves in green ribbon.

Roses: With floss, work five-legged star as base. With medium pink ribbon begin weaving over and under legs of star, then use light pink to finish. Work a dark pink French knot at center of rose. With ribbon, work French

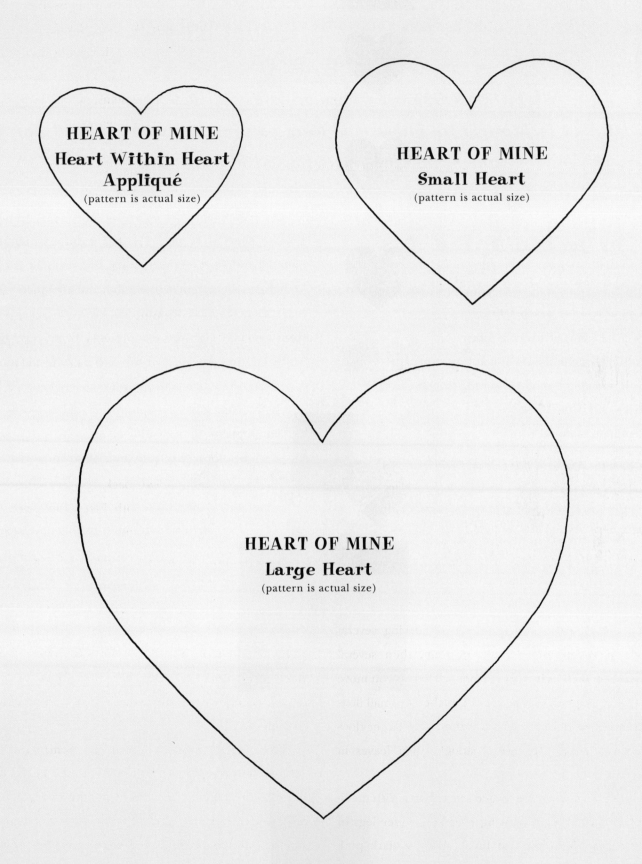

HEART OF MINE
Heart Within Heart
Appliqué
(pattern is actual size)

HEART OF MINE
Small Heart
(pattern is actual size)

HEART OF MINE
Large Heart
(pattern is actual size)

TOY SOLDIERS

Whether parading two by two or six by six, these charming soldiers in their bright red jackets and black hats trimmed with gold will march straight into the heart of a special little child.

materials

- ½ yd (46cm) each of red, black, white, and gray fabric
- ¼ yd (23cm) of peach fabric
- 1¾ yds (1.5m) of backing fabric
- Batting (Fairfield Soft Touch Cotton)
- Gold metallic thread for sewing machine use
- Black and white thread
- Templatc material

Note: You may choose to assemble this quilt as shown here, cutting fewer pieces and sewing into corners, or you may choose to make use of the supplementary lines and thus avoid sewing into corners.

Enlarge pattern on page 115 and transfer to template material adding ¼" (6mm) seam allowances all around. To make as shown, cut eighteen hat and boot pieces from black, eighteen faces from peach, eighteen jacket pieces from red and eighteen pant pieces from gray. From white, cut thirty-six each of top and bottom side pieces.

Using ¼" (6mm) seams, sew the pieces together into blocks. Assemble the completed soldier blocks into three strips of six soldiers each. Sew the strips together, lining up seam lines between blocks.

Lay backing out right side down on flat surface. Smooth batting over backing. Center quilt top, right side up, onto batting and backing.

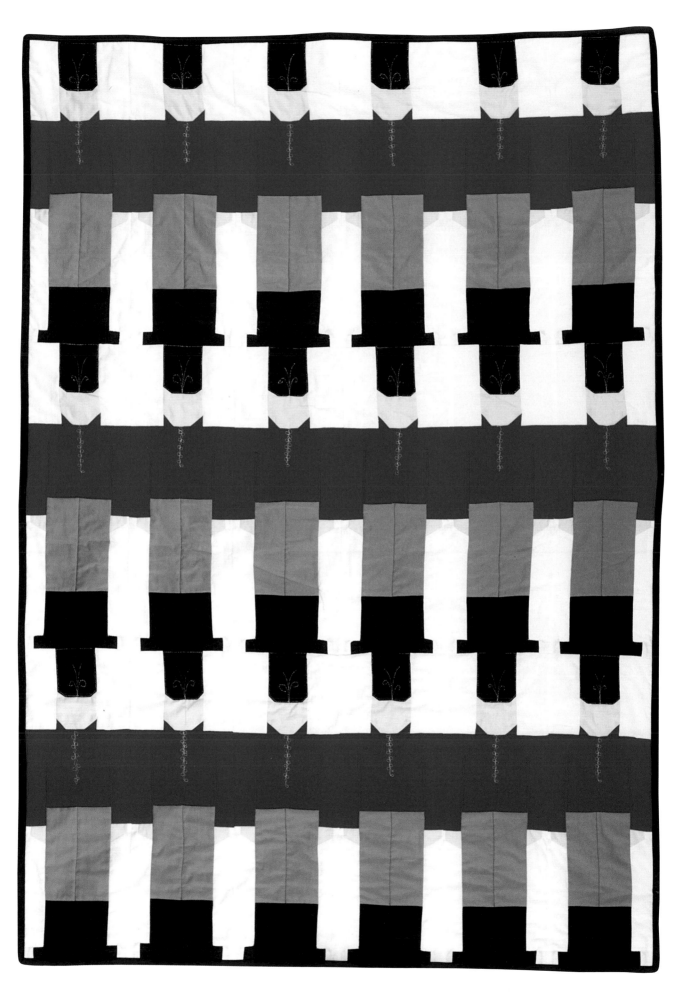

Baste layers together. With machine threaded on top with black thread, quilt on the red, close to edges all around outside of jackets and between arm and body to within 1" (2.5cm) of shoulder. Quilt down the center of pants and boots. Replace the top thread with gold metallic thread and quilt close to the edges around each hat, then work the design motifs on each hat. Set the machine for a decorative stitch and work down the center of each jacket to within 1½" (4cm) of bottom edge. If your machine does not have a suitable decorative stitch, work a zigzag stitch down and back to create a row of small diamonds. If desired, you may also quilt around sides and bottoms of boots, pants, and around the hands and faces using white or nylon thread. Trim batting and backing even with quilt top.

From remaining black fabric, cut four binding strips, two 1¾" × 40" (4.5 × 102cm) and two 1¾" × 58" (4.5 × 147cm), piecing if necessary. Fold strips in half lengthwise and having raw edges even, pin to right side of quilt leaving at least 1" (2.5cm) excess at each end. Using a ¼" (6mm) seam, sew binding strips to quilt, starting and ending ¼" (6mm) from edges of quilt. Miter the corners of adjoining binding strips. Turn folded edge to back and slipstitch fold in place just over seam line.

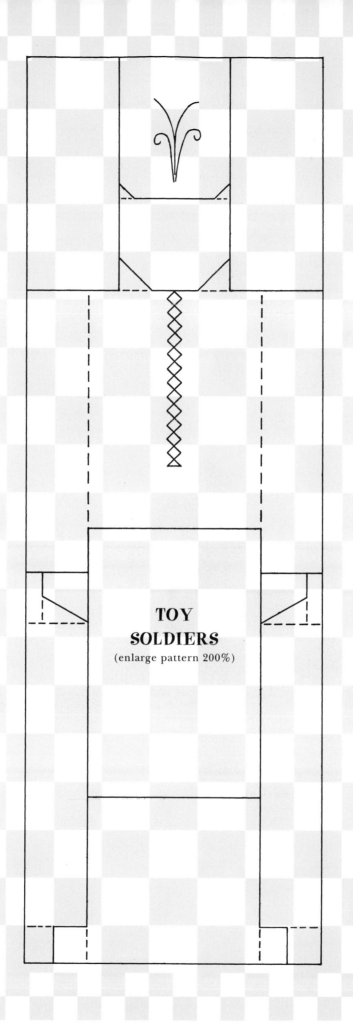

TOY
SOLDIERS
(enlarge pattern 200%)

SOURCES

Allian Trim Inc.
1500 Seneca Run
Ambler, PA 19002
1-800-551-2569
(215) 654-1555

C.M. Offray & Son, Inc.
Route 24, Box 601
Chester, NJ 07930-0601

Country Appliqués
P.O. Box 7109
Shawnee Mission, KS 66207
(913) 491-1237

Creative Textiles
380 East Austin Street
New Braunfels, TX 78131
1-800-628-2513
(212) 494-0110

Delaware D.G. Co.
1007 South Chapel Street
Newark, DE 19702
1-800-444-7300
(302) 731-0500

Fabric Barn
3121 East Anaheim Street
Long Beach, CA 90804
(310) 498-0285

Harvest Import Inc.
1414 East Katella Avenue
Anaheim, CA 92805
(714) 939-1096

SOURCES (CONTINUED)

Joan Toggitt Ltd.
2 Riverview Drive
Somerset, NJ 08873-1139
(908) 271-1949

L & L Lace Company
218 South Brindlee Mountain Parkway
Arab, AL 35016
1-800-828-0033

Plus One, Inc.
969 Industrial Road, Suite E
San Carlos, CA 94070
1-800-697-4226

Springs Industry Inc.
Retail Fabrics Division
420 West White Street, Box 6548
Rock Hill, SC 29730

WFR Ribbon Inc.
95 Mayhill Street
Saddle Brook, NJ 07662
1-800-883-7700

The Yarn Barn
4300 McCullough
San Antonio, TX 78212
1-800-527-7125